Yourself

Read and write Chinese script

Elizabeth Scurfield
and
Song Lianyi

For UK order enquiries: please contact Bookpoint Ltd, 130 Milton Park, Abingdon, Oxon OX14 4SB. Telephone: +44 (0) 1235 827720. Fax: +44 (0) 1235 400454. Lines are open 09.00–17.00, Monday to Saturday, with a 24-hour message answering service. Details about our titles and how to order are available at www.teachyourself.com

For USA order enquiries: please contact McGraw-Hill Customer Services, PO Box 545, Blacklick, OH 43004-0545, USA. Telephone: 1-800-722-4726. Fax: 1-614-755-5645.

For Canada order enquiries: please contact McGraw-Hill Ryerson Ltd, 300 Water St, Whitby, Ontario L1N 9B6, Canada. Telephone: 905 430 5000. Fax: 905 430 5020.

Long renowned as the authoritative source for self-guided learning – with more than 50 million copies sold worldwide – the **Teach Yourself** series includes over 500 titles in the fields of languages, crafts, hobbies, business, computing and education.

British Library Cataloguing in Publication Data: a catalogue record for this title is available from the British Library.

Library of Congress Catalog Card Number: on file.

First published in UK 1999 as *Teach Yourself Beginner's Chinese Script* by Hodder Education, part of Hachette UK, 338 Euston Road, London NW1 3BH.

First published in US 1999 by The McGraw-Hill Companies, Inc.

This edition published 2010.

The **Teach Yourself** name is a registered trade mark of Hachette UK.

Typeset by MPS Limited, a Macmillan Company.

Printed in Great Britain for Hodder Education, an Hachette UK Company, 338 Euston Road, London NW1 3BH.

The publisher has used its best endeavours to ensure that the URLs for external websites referred to in this book are correct and active at the time of going to press. However, the publisher and the authors have no responsibility for the websites and can make no guarantee that a site will remain live or that the content will remain relevant, decent or appropriate.

Hachette UK's policy is to use papers that are natural, renewable and recyclable products and made from wood grown in sustainable forests. The logging and manufacturing processes are expected to conform to the environmental regulations of the country of origin.

Impression number 10 9 8 7 6 5 4 3 2 1

Year 2014 2013 2012 2011 2010

Contents

Dedications

To my partner, Martina Weitsch, who has pilot-tested the exercises in this book and made a host of helpful suggestions.

To Kelin, my daughter, who has inspired me throughout the production of this book.

Acknowledgements

Our grateful thanks to all those who made this publication possible. In particular we wish to thank our editor, Virginia Catmur, for all her encouragement and support.

Meet the authors

Elizabeth Scurfield and Song Lianyi are both experienced and enthusiastic teachers of Chinese. Elizabeth Scurfield graduated with a first-class honours degree in Chinese from the School of Oriental and African Studies in London and has taught Chinese for nearly 40 years, 30 of them at university level. She was co-founder of the Chinese Department at the University of Westminster (1974) at the age of 23 and brought new ideas and enthusiasm to its creation. She has made numerous short and extended visits and study trips to China since her first visit in 1976 as the only woman participant on a delegation of younger sinologists.

Song Lianyi (Song being the surname) grew up in China. He obtained his BA in China and his MA and PhD in the UK. Currently he is Principal Teaching Fellow in Chinese at the School of Oriental and African Studies, University of London, where he has taught Chinese for over 15 years. He has been an active member of the British Chinese Language Teaching Society and is a life member of the International Society for Chinese Language Teaching.

Elizabeth Scurfield and Song Lianyi were colleagues in the same university nearly 20 years ago and their fruitful collaboration has continued ever since. In addition to *Read and write Chinese script*, their current titles in the *Teach Yourself* series include *Speak Mandarin Chinese with confidence* and *Get started in Mandarin Chinese*.

Elizabeth Scurfield and Song Lianyi

Only got a minute?

Chinese, in one form or another, is spoken by more people around the globe than any other language and China is now starting to claim a major role for itself in the global economy. For these reasons alone, it is worthwhile trying to learn at least a little of the language. It is also the world's oldest language still in use and its cultural history can be traced back over 3,500 years. Mandarin Chinese, which you will be learning in this course, is the Chinese language with the most speakers; and even those Chinese for whom Mandarin is not the mother tongue will be proficient in Mandarin, as it is the dominant language of the People's Republic of China. It is also the main language of Taiwan and one of the official languages in Singapore.

The characters used in this book are always in the simplified script except for one or two full-form (traditional) characters, which are to be found in various signs and notices. Simplified characters are used in the People's Republic of China, Singapore and increasingly in overseas Chinese communities. They are commonly taught to foreign students learning Chinese. In Hong Kong, while more and more people are learning to speak Modern Standard Chinese ('putonghua'), full-form characters are still in use: simplified characters have not yet been officially adopted.

While you may have an idea that Mandarin will be a difficult language to learn, this is not necessarily true. Its grammar is remarkably simple and regular. For example, there is only ever one form of the verb, unlike in English, where we have *to be, am, is, are, was, were, will be* . . . In Mandarin one verb form covers all these functions. Some learners worry that they won't be able to learn the 'tones' of Mandarin: but if you learn the tone every time you learn a new word, you will soon find that you produce the correct tone automatically. Even if your tones are not brilliant, people can still understand you fairly easily when they are actually speaking with you.

We hope that, with the aid of this course, you should have a decent grounding in reading and writing Chinese script and that, by the end of the course, you will have the confidence to give it a go when you go to China, whether for business or pleasure.

10 Only got ten minutes?

The Chinese language

Chinese can now be considered as very much an international language and is one of the six official languages of the United Nations, alongside Arabic, English, French, Russian and Spanish. With over 1.4 billion mother tongue speakers spread across the globe, Chinese is quite possibly the fastest growing spoken language in the world, in terms of numbers. In addition to its being an official language of the UN (and, obviously, in China itself), Chinese is also the official language in Hong Kong (with the spoken language being Cantonese of course, rather than Mandarin, with English as the other official language), Taiwan and Macau (with Portuguese the other official language) and one of the four official languages spoken in Singapore (but it is not the main language in this country). It is recognized as a regional language in Malaysia and, interestingly enough, in the United States of America. The large immigrant population is obviously the reason for this and it can be seen that similar immigrant populations to other parts of the globe are having the same sort of effect.

Spoken Chinese has a high level of internal diversity and even though all spoken regional varieties have tonality in common, the number of tones may differ. There are generally considered to be around 13 main dialectic or language groups (even this distinction is controversial) but the language that is spoken by the most people by far is the language we are going to be learning in this course: Mandarin Chinese, which is spoken as a mother tongue by approximately 900 million people. Other groupings include Wu and Cantonese, the latter being spoken by between 60–70 million people. Furthermore, it is usually thought that these main groupings are mutually unintelligible.

Chinese as it is spoken within China shows huge variations, as we have just seen, from north to south, west to east. It is, therefore, to be expected that there is no one form of Chinese when it is spoken as the main language in another country (see earlier for these other countries) – each of these countries has its own dialect and once more we find that even within these countries, there are marked differences from one region to another, whether this be accent, pronunciation or more marked and profound differences that might render a speaker of one dialect not understood by a speaker of another.

With China's expansion into the global market, the numbers of non-Chinese people, businesspeople and other people alike, who are turning to the learning of Chinese as an essential medium of communication for the future, are booming. With so much manufacturing taking place in China nowadays and outsourcing of other industries and with China now becoming one of the world's leading economies, it makes enormous sense for Westerners to learn at least the basics of Chinese, because protocols are very different from those of the West and, if we wish to avoid antagonizing our friends, business colleagues and other people, these protocols must be learned, too.

Of course, there are so many native speakers of Chinese because of the size of the Chinese population: some 1.4 billion worldwide. Until fairly recently, Chinese government policy included a 'one child' requirement for families, in order to try and keep population growth within bounds. This requirement has now been dropped and the expectation is, therefore, that China's population will swell even more rapidly. Another reason to learn some Chinese, because you will have many more people to practise your language skills with!

So, we can see that globalization, international trade and, now, tourism have all played a huge role in contributing to the continuing and wide spread of Chinese – and, of course, Beijing's staging the Olympic Games in 2008 boosted China's image on the worldwide stage, in addition to its possessing some of the most famous tourist attractions in the world (the Great Wall being but one).

Written documentation on the development of Chinese goes back for nearly four centuries, making Chinese the oldest language on the planet. And, as the speakers of the language have developed and changed over this time, so, too, has the language itself. Probably the main change would be the apparent simplification of the form of the language, resulting in the 'alphabet' (i.e. character set) consisting of a mere 400 or so syllables. And yet, the language continues to be vibrant and evolving, due to the extensions possible through compounding and tonal additions.

Other languages spoken in China

We have mentioned that, in addition to regional variations and dialects, there are several other actual languages spoken in China – although Mandarin is spoken by the overwhelming majority of the population. The second language, in terms of numbers speaking it, is Wu, which is estimated to be spoken by anywhere between 90 and 100 million, e.g. in Shanghai and surrounding regions, Min, spoken by a further 60–70 million (estimated number, e.g. in Fujian Province and Taiwan) and, the other language you have undoubtedly heard of, Cantonese, which is also spoken by approximately 60–70 million people (e.g. in Hong Kong and Guangdong Province). Then there are two reasonably widespread languages that are spoken in China, namely, Xiang and Hakka, although, as we referred to briefly earlier, there is some controversy as to whether these constitute languages as such or whether they are really dialects. Xiang (known also as Hunanese, as it is spoken predominantly, but not exclusively, in Hunan Province) is a language that has been profoundly influenced by Mandarin and is spoken by about 35–40 million people in Hunan and also Sichuan Province. (It may be of interest to know that Mao Zedong was born in Hunan Province and belief has it that, although a native speaker of Xiang, he was not at all fluent in Mandarin!) Hakka is spoken mainly in the south of China and was originally confined to the Hakka people, but is now also predominant in Taiwan and in Chinese immigrant populations around the world (very approximate numbers of Hakka speakers 35–40 million).

Chinese characters: the essentials

The fundamental building block of the Chinese language is the character, a single-syllable morpheme whereby each individual character forms one idea. And there are in the region of 400 of these basic monosyllables in Chinese – when these individual 'cells' of the language are combined, they form homophones, in which Chinese abounds. Unfortunately, this is what adds to the complicated nature of the language. This difficulty (for us as learners of Chinese) is ameliorated somewhat by Chinese's being a tonal language. *Putonghua* has four tones, so our original paltry 400-odd monosyllables become over 1,400 different sounds (as some sound plus tone combinations do not exist) in one fell swoop. But also the characters that in Chinese we find combined in this way have similar meanings when used to form the new 'word' – confusion here is avoided since, when used separately, individual characters may take on another meaning; in combination, they can usually only mean one thing.

Most syllables in Chinese consist of two elements: an initial and a final, the former being a consonant at the beginning of the syllable and the latter, the rest of the syllable.

The characters used in this book are always in the simplified script except for one or two full-form (traditional) characters, which are to be found in various signs and notices. Simplified characters are used in the People's Republic of China, Singapore and increasingly in overseas Chinese communities. They are commonly taught to foreign students learning Chinese. In Hong Kong, while more and more people are learning to speak Modern Standard Chinese (*putonghua*), full-form characters are still in use: simplified characters have not yet been officially adopted.

Initials

There are some 21 initials in Modern Standard Chinese (MSC); the semi-vowels 'w' and 'y' are considered by some to be initials, too. In addition, there is 'ng', a sound that occurs at the end of a syllable, as the same sound does in English. These sounds include six aspirated initials and six unaspirated initials, all 12 of which are voiceless. When making an aspirated sound, a feather or a sheet of paper held in front of your mouth will move; when making an unaspirated one, it should not. Lack of vibration in your vocal chords renders the initial voiceless.

Finals

Chinese has 36 finals, which are composed of a simple or compound vowel or a vowel plus a nasal consonant. Some syllables may lack the initial consonant but none lack a vowel.

Tones

The four tones in Chinese (remember from our earlier discussion that their presence multiplies the number of possible sounds available to about 1,400) are variations in pitch – rising, continuing and falling. Each syllable in the language has its own specific tone, so they are an important component in 'word' formation.

The first tone is high and level, the second is rising, the third tone is a short fall followed by a rising tone and the fourth tone is a falling tone. (Note, however, that you do not have to produce a particular sort of sound in your own speech – all the tones occur naturally within the voice range.)

There is also a neutral tone, i.e. the syllable is toneless: all particles are neutral, the second half of a repeated word may be in neutral tone, fill-in syllables are neutral and the second syllable in a compound may be neutral (but on other occasions, not, so this neutrality has to be indicated in the text). One example is **xièxie**, *thank you*.

In the spoken language, you will find that it is rare for tones to be given their full value, but this doesn't let you off the hook! You should still learn them as if they were and, also, be aware that learning the words with their tone takes time, practice and lots of listening and repetition on your part. So do persevere!

Some additional points

Here are a few little extras, to cheer you up as you are about to embark on this course – it's all in the mind, you know:

One way in which to ask questions in Chinese is to use both positive and negative forms of the verb together. And then the corresponding answer is neither yes nor no but either the positive or negative form of that verb.

As you know by now, Chinese does not have a phonetic alphabet and *pinyin* is the nearest we in the West get to a recognizable form of transcribing it. It will be very useful for you in this course, as it provides a relatively accurate guide to correct pronunciation.

Where names in the West appear in the form title, given name, surname, in Chinese, they appear totally the other way around, viz. surname, given name, title. Hence, Mao, to whom we referred earlier on in this section, is the Chinese leader's surname and Zedong is actually his given name.

Some adjectives function as verbs, a form known as *stative verbs*, meaning that, in a 'to be' verb, there is no need for the 'to be' bit of it.

Unlike in English, an adverb will always go in front of the verb it is qualifying.

One feature of the language that should please you immensely (especially if you have learned other languages in the past or if English is not your first language and you have had to struggle with this aspect) is that all verbs are invariable – meaning that they remain exactly the same, no matter what else is going on! Another feature of verbs that you will like is that (with one exception – the verb *to have* **yǒu**) negation comes through the use of **bù**, which precedes the verb.

We hope that this short introduction has kindled that spark of interest that led you to pick up this book in the first place.

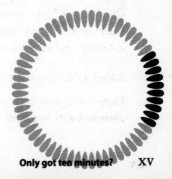

Introduction

Most people take one look at the Chinese script and say 'Oh no, I couldn't possibly learn that, it's much too complicated' or perhaps 'I'm no good at drawing so I wouldn't be able to write Chinese'. By the time you get to the end of this book you will have realized that neither of these statements is true. You may decide that you have not got the *time* to learn the Chinese script but that is a different matter. Anybody of average intelligence and with a reasonable visual memory who is prepared to put in the necessary time *can* master the Chinese script.

The Chinese script is an amazing tool with which you will be able to go some way towards understanding Chinese, one of the world's most ancient languages, and its culture.

Read and write Chinese script starts from scratch, explaining the origins of the language and how characters have evolved. It teaches you how to write characters correctly from the beginning and, through a series of carefully graded exercises, how to understand enough from signs, directions, instructions and even menus to be able to get by. You will surprise yourself with your ingenuity and your ability to guess correctly, based on the sound logic learnt from this book.

The characters used in this book are always in the simplified script except for one or two full-form (traditional) characters, which are to be found in various signs and notices. Simplified characters are used in the People's Republic of China, Singapore and increasingly in overseas Chinese communities. They are commonly taught to foreign students learning Chinese. In Hong Kong, while more and more people are learning to speak Modern Standard Chinese (*putonghua*), full-form characters are still in use: simplified characters have not yet been officially adopted.

This book is to be enjoyed, with many examples taken from real life. By the time you have finished it, we hope you will have caught the Chinese bug – hours of enjoyment (and hard work) lie ahead of you!

How to use the book

The book is divided into two main parts. Units 1–4 introduce you to the origins of the Chinese script and explain how characters and words are formed and the basic rules in writing them.

Units 5–9 introduce you to real-life situations such as reading signs, maps, notices and even menus. You will be able to write numbers and dates, tell the time and fill out simple forms. There is a Mini-test following Units 4 and 9.

Unit 10 explains how to use a Chinese–English dictionary and Chinese word-processing packages with concrete examples. There is also a brief introduction to Chinese idioms. While at the beginning of the book we provide spaces for you to write your answers into the book, you should really work with a notebook alongside you, where you can practise writing Chinese characters and make your own notes to help you remember what you've learned.

At the back of the book

At the back of the book there is a reference section which contains:

- a **Taking it further** section to encourage you to extend your skills in Chinese
- a **Key to the exercises**
- a **Table of radicals** for easy reference
- a **Guide to pronunciation and tones**
- **Useful public signs and notices**
- a **Chinese–English vocabulary** list containing all the characters in the course, listed according to radical and with the number of the unit where they first occurred
- an **English–Chinese vocabulary** list containing all the most important words which have occurred in the course

1

....

Origins of the script

In this unit you will learn:

- What the earliest characters looked like
- About the evolution of characters over the years
- Ten basic characters

Many ancient peoples wrote in symbols, including the Chinese. The most well known are perhaps Egyptian hieroglyphics carved on stone or written on papyrus. What was common to all the known ancient scripts was that at their earliest form of development they consisted of picture signs, many of which looked quite similar.

The differences, however, are also striking. Look at two of the signs for water for instance (third column from right). The Egyptian sign seems to represent calm water, whereas the Chinese sign indicates a winding river flooding its banks, which is just what the Yellow River (known as the cradle of Chinese civilization) used to do.

We still use symbols or signs today as a kind of international language which overcomes communication barriers on a very basic but necessary level.

Exercise 1

What do the following signs mean?

a _____ b _____ c _____ d _____

e _____ f _____ g _____

The earliest examples of written Chinese are found on the oracle bones used in divination rites in the Shang dynasty (c1500BC–1066BC). Nearly 2,500 separate characters have been found on bone fragments dating back to this period, so the total in use must have been much greater than this. Of these characters, approximately 600 have been identified.

These are characters appearing on oracle bones. They are very different from the writing of today.

The first step in building up a written language in China was the use of pictured objects or pictographs to represent the objects themselves. About 10% of all characters in modern Chinese come from these pictographs. Here are a few examples of pictographs showing the evolution of some characters into their present form. The earliest form of the character is on the left, the one used today (hand-written) is on the extreme right.

⊙　⊖　⊟　日　*rì*　sun

𝖣　𝔻　夕　月　*yuè*　moon

？　勹　几　人　*rén*　person

米　米　朩　木　*mù*　wood/tree

···

Insight

Although simplified characters were officially adopted in the People's Republic of China in the 1950s, simplification of Chinese writing had been going on over hundreds of years. Such simplification mainly manifested itself in different styles of calligraphy. Look at the following styles of calligraphy and you will notice the differences.

Here are five common scripts in Chinese writing. It's the character for 'bird'.

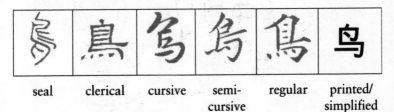

| seal | clerical | cursive | semi-cursive | regular | printed/simplified |

(*Source*: http://www.rice-paper.com/uses/calligraphy.html)

Here is another example, the character for 'horse', in the same five styles.

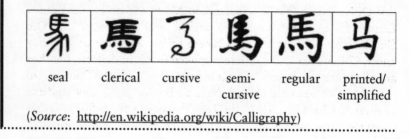

| seal | clerical | cursive | semi-cursive | regular | printed/simplified |

(*Source*: http://en.wikipedia.org/wiki/Calligraphy)

Exercise 2

Match up the pictured objects in column 1 with the old forms of the pictograph in columns 2 and 3 and the modern-day form (printed) in column 4 (simplified characters in brackets). Write the numbers in the space provided in the last column, for example: **1A 2B 3C 4D**. Then check your answers in the **Key to the exercises**.

	1	2	3	4	
A				車(车)	_____ **4A**
B				馬(马)	_____ **4B**
C				魚(鱼)	_____ **4C**
D				雨	_____ **4D**
E				山	_____ **4E**
F				子	_____ **4F**

Why did the ancient Chinese writing system survive, while that of the Egyptians, Hittites or Sumerians did not? One of the major reasons must be that China was unified at a very early stage in history by the first Qin emperor, Qin Shi Huangdi, in 221BC and unlike the Roman Empire, for example, has stayed unified until the present day. Qin Shi Huangdi also unified the Chinese script. As some of you may know, Chinese has many different spoken forms or dialects, but they are all written in exactly the same way, so all literate Chinese can read the same newspapers and the same books. Japan sent students to study in China as early as the Tang dynasty (AD618–907), so that when the Japanese started to keep written records they 'borrowed' Chinese characters, which are still in use in modern written Japanese and are referred to as *kanji*. The Koreans did the same thing although modern Korean contains no Chinese characters.

Exercise 3

See if you can remember or work out what the characters below mean. Don't worry if you can't; you can always check your answers in the **Key to the exercises**.

1 月	2 木	3 山	4 雨	5 日
6 鱼	7 马	8 车	9 子	10 人

Insight

Simplified characters were introduced in the People's Republic of China after 1949. The purpose was to enable the population, who were largely illiterate, to learn the characters more easily. Even though in the early 1950s Chairman Mao advocated the use of romanization to replace characters, this has never happened to any significant extent. The use of romanization (transcribing Chinese sounds into the Latin script) is mainly confined to some brand names, company names, shop signs and street signs, where it appears above or below the Chinese characters.

Generally speaking, the Chinese script, unlike most European languages, is not a phonetic language in that one cannot be certain as to how to pronounce a character without actually learning its pronunciation. It is not surprising that the Chinese themselves can't pronounce characters which they have not learned. In English, for example, one can read an unseen new word with a reasonable amount of accuracy.

This, however, does not mean that characters do not contain any phonetic clues. In fact, many do. This will be explained in the next unit.

Points to remember

- Although quite a few characters originated from early drawings and are thus termed 'pictographs', modern day characters no longer resemble the objects they were originally meant to portray. However, it is still interesting to know what these characters looked like in their early forms.
- While the distinction between simplified and traditional scripts is obvious, one has to remember that many characters remain the same in both sets of script.

Test yourself

1 Where is traditional Chinese script (characters) used?
   a the People's Republic of China   **b** Hong Kong
   c Taiwan

2 Which character has the shape of a vertical rectangle with a horizontal line in the middle?
   a the sun   **b** the moon   **c** mountain

3 Which of the two characters is 'human' or 'person'?
   a 入   **b** 人

4 What is the simplified character for the traditional character 'vehicle' 車?
   a 木   **b** 鱼   **c** 车

5 What is the traditional character for 'horse' 马?
   a 馬   **b** 鱼   **c** 車

How Chinese characters are formed

In this unit you will learn:

- What radicals are
- Various ways in which characters are composed
- More than 30 new characters/radicals

In Unit 1, we saw how characters evolved from drawings of objects to what they look like today. Drawings, however vivid they might be, are not sufficient to express more complex concepts and ideas, especially more abstract ones. Over the years, these **pictographs** were extended or combined to form **ideographs**. 'Two people' on top of the character for 'earth' meant 'to sit' 坐; a 'woman' 女 with a 'child' 子 beside her meant 'good' 好; a 'pig' 豕 under a 'roof' 宀 meant 'home' 家, etc.

Try the following exercise and see if you can work out what these ancient ideographs are trying to express.

Exercise 1

Write out the meaning of the following characters or ideographs. The components of each character are presented with their meaning. You have already seen some of the components in Unit 1. Most of them are meaningful characters in their own right.

Meaning

囚	人 person	口	enclosure	
明	日 sun	月	moon	_____

坐	人	person	土	earth	_____
休	人*	person	木	tree	_____
男	田	field	力	strength	_____

*In combination 人 becomes 亻 on the left-hand side.

Now let's see if you have understood them correctly. A 'person' in an 'enclosure' is a 'prisoner'. 'Sun' and 'moon' together means 'bright'. And as we just saw, 'two people' 'down to earth' means 'to sit'. When a 'person' is against a 'tree', s/he is 'resting'. The 'strength' in the 'field' comes from a 'man' or a 'male'. Do these make sense to you?

The following characters are composed in the same way as those in Exercise 1. Let's see if you can work out their meanings. Remember these characters were made a long time ago. The concepts in those days might not always be the same as we perceive them today. For instance, why is it 'good' to have a child? Because in traditional Chinese society, as in many others around the world, a child, and more particularly a male child, was necessary to carry on the family line and to worship the ancestors. Children were (and are) also necessary to work in the fields, particularly in the labour-intensive paddy fields.

Insight

It helps you to memorize characters if you can perceive and remember their components. In this unit, we have illustrated 'meaning' components and 'sound' components of characters. There are, of course, components which do not fall into either category. It is still helpful if you treat each component as a building block rather than as a combination of individual strokes.

Exercise 2

Write out the meaning of the following characters in the space provided.

					Meaning
信	亻	person	言	speech/words	_____
鲜	鱼	fish	羊	sheep	_____
安	宀	roof	女	woman	_____

A person's words convey a 'message' or can be passed on in writing as a 'letter'. Fish and sheep's meat must be eaten when they are 'fresh'. Once there is a woman in a household, there will be a family, which brings 'stability', hence the meaning of 'safe' and 'secure'.

Did you get any of them right? If you did, well done! If you didn't, it's not surprising at this stage. These meanings may be very obscure to the beginner but they tell us a lot about traditional Chinese values such as the importance of the family and of having a male heir.

Word building was not just a matter of putting two pictographs together. This method would still not have created enough new characters to convey many of the ideas and concepts which exist in a developed language. Another method of creating new characters which dated after the Shang dynasty (c1500–1066BC) is sometimes called the **phonogram**. It is made up of two components, one of which is usually known as the **radical** and the other the **phonetic**, which gives a clue as to the character's pronunciation.

What is a radical?

A radical is a component of a character. It sometimes gives us a partial idea of the meaning of the whole character. Just as the Greek prefix 'phil' tells us that the word has something to do with 'love' (*phil*anthropy is the love of humankind, a *phil*osopher is a lover of wisdom etc.), when a Chinese sees a character with the 'heart' radical, written 心 or 忄 depending on its position, s/he can assume that the character has something to do with the emotions. For example, 愛 means 'love; to love', 恨 means 'hate; to hate', 怕 means 'to fear'.

Each character has at least one radical. Some characters are built up of radicals only, but in these cases, one or more of the radicals is acting as the phonetic in that particular character. Let's look at the character 想 *xiǎng* which means 'to miss' or 'think of' (a person or thing) or just 'to think'. It is made up of the 'heart' radical 心 and two other radicals, 木 'wood/tree' and 目 'eye', but in this case, when 木 and 目 are put together 相, they are pronounced *xiāng* and they provide the phonetic component for the character 想.

Another example is the character 江 *jiāng*, 'river', which is made up of the 'water' radical 氵 and the radical *gōng* 工, meaning 'work'. From the meaning of the character, 'river', 工 is obviously the phonetic element here although it is not particularly helpful as the sound has changed so much.

As you can see from all of this, radicals are *not* equivalent to letters in English. All radicals mean something in themselves, but this does not always help with the meaning of the character as a whole. For instance, the fact that the radical for a particular character is a dot ` or a horizontal or vertical line 一 丨 helps us to find it in the dictionary but gives us no indication of the meaning of the character whatsoever.

Here is a table of some single- or two-stroke radicals which do not necessarily carry any meaning. The ones with meaning that you have met so far are listed in a table at the end of this unit. Refer to the radical table at the end of the book for a fuller list.

| 、 一 丨 丿 乛 乙 乛 乚 儿 |
| 厂 匚 卜 冂 厂 乂 勹 凵 厶 |

There are around 190–230 radicals in Chinese writing. The discrepancy in numbers results from how some of the radicals are grouped and the inclusion or exclusion of some of the complicated ones. At the beginning of a Chinese dictionary there is usually an index of radicals. The characters in the dictionary are based on the index. In Unit 10 we will show you how to look up a character in a Chinese dictionary.

How are characters formed?

There are a number of ways in which characters are formed. The examples in Exercises 1 and 2 represent one of the most common ways: combining the meanings of two radicals to form a new meaning. The following are some more examples of this.

Radical + radical

竹* bamboo + 毛 fur/hair = 笔 Chinese writing brush
言* speech + 舌 tongue = 话 words, speech; to speak

小　small + 大 big　= 尖 sharp, pointed
日　sun　+ 月 moon = 明 bright

*Note that 言 becomes 讠 when acting as the radical on the left-hand side of a simplified character, and 竹 becomes ⺮ when acting as the radical on top of a character.

As you may have observed, the position of a radical in a character varies. It can be on the left or right side of a character, or it can be on the top or bottom of a character. It can also be on the inside or outside of a character. It is important to know where a particular radical occurs in a character so that you can identify it and be able to look it up in the dictionary (more on this later). The radical's actual position normally has no bearing on the meaning or interpretation of the character.

竹 bamboo, for instance, always occurs on the top of a character when it looks like ⺮, as does 草 grass, when it looks like ⺿. Fire 火 can occur on the left-hand side of a character as 火 or on the bottom of a character when it looks like ⺣. The radical for speech 言 appears on the left-hand side of a character and is written as 讠 when it is simplified.

Exercise 3

You know 人 means 'person', 木 means 'wood/tree' and 火 means 'fire'. What do you think the following characters mean?

Radicals	Character(s)	Meaning
人 + 人	= 从*	_____
人 + 人 + 人	= 众*	_____
木 + 木	= 林	_____
木 + 木 + 木	= 森	_____
火 + 火	= 炎	_____
火 + 火 + 火	= 焱	_____

*These are simplified characters. The principle of making characters, however, remains the same.

In some combinations, as in Exercise 3, the meaning is very clear to the Westerner (at least after it has been given!), but in others it remains very obscure. It is important to be aware that there is not a consistent logic inherent in the formation of all Chinese characters, so that although we can see in some of today's characters how they have developed from their earliest forms, there is no methodology which will serve us for them all. In addition, concepts have changed. Pigs 豕 are rarely kept under the same roof as their owners, but 家 'pig under a roof' still means 'home'; villages are seldom made of wood these days, but the character for village 村 still has 木 'wood/tree' as its radical.

You may well ask: but how do we know how to pronounce these characters? The answer is we don't, at least not for sure in most cases. Unlike languages with an alphabet, Chinese characters do not directly indicate the pronunciation. However, you will find a brief guide to pronunciation at the back of the book.

Radical + phonetic

We have already looked at how the Chinese expanded their written vocabulary by putting two pictograms or two radicals together. The next most common method is what we may call the **radical + phonetic** method or **phonogram**, which we referred to earlier. The following examples are composed of two parts: a radical conveying meaning and a phonetic element. Although when standing alone, these phonetic elements carry meaning and may or may not be radicals, here they perform the function of indicating the sound to some extent. In the examples which follow, the phonetic or sound element *does* indicate the sound of the whole character, but this is the exception rather the rule. In most cases, characters with the same phonetic element are pronounced slightly differently and mostly in a different tone. (There are four tones in Modern Standard Chinese or Mandarin, seven in Cantonese. Our point of reference in this book is Modern Standard Chinese which is understood by about 70% of the Chinese population.)

You may notice in the following examples that the characters for 'far' and 'garden' share the same phonetic component. They do sound similar, although one is in the second tone indicated by ´ and the other is in the third tone indicated by ˇ . The characters for 'to accompany' and 'to blend' also share the same sound radical and they are pronounced exactly the same, with the same tone, in this case fourth ` .

Sound	Meaning	(Meaning) radical	Sound
远 *yuǎn*	far	辶 (to walk quickly)	元 (*yuán*)
碗 *wǎn*	bowl	石 (stone, mineral)	宛 (*wǎn*)
们 *men**	persons	人 (person)	门 (*mén*)
伴 *bàn*	to accompany	人 (person)	半 (*bàn*)
拌 *bàn*	to blend	扌 (hand)	半 (*bàn*)
订 *dìng*	to book	言 (speech)	丁 (*dīng*)
钉 *dīng*	nail	钅 (metal)	丁 (*dīng*)
锈 *xiù*	rusty	钅 (metal)	秀 (*xiù*)
吐 *tǔ*	to spit	口 (mouth)	土 (*tǔ*)
园 *yuán*	garden	囗 (enclosure)	元 (*yuán*)
房 *fáng*	house	户 (household)	方 (*fāng*)
骑 *qí**	to ride (a horse)	马 (horse)	奇 (*qí*)

*Check the pronunciation at the back of the book. It is *not* the same as in English.

By looking at the position of the radicals in the examples in this section and in characters or references earlier in the unit, you should be able to do the next two exercises.

Exercise 4

In each of the characters that follow, the radical is missing. (We have written it in the first column for you.) Where does it go? On the top, on the bottom, on the left-hand side or on the right-hand side?

Radicals

1 马 (horse) 累 (mule) 户 (donkey) 句 (pony)
2 艹 (grass) 化 (flower) 早 (grass) 牙 (sprouts)
3 钅 (metal) 冈 (steel) 秀 (rusty) 令 (bell)
4 辶 (to walk) 兆 (escape) 寸 (to pass) 万 (to step over)

Exercise 5

Which character is right? Circle the correct one.

1 to hit   忊 打 订   2 stove   灶 杜 吐
3 to scorn 饥 机 讯   4 snow   雪 扫 灵

Let's summarize the radicals you have seen in these first two units. More radicals will be introduced in Units 3–5. A complete table of radicals will be found in the reference section at the back of the book.

车	vehicle	鱼	fish	木	tree	水 氵	water
宀	roof	大	big	毛	hair, fur	人 亻	person
雨	rain	子	child	土	earth	心 忄	heart
田	field	力	strength	羊	sheep	言 讠	speech
石	stone	日	sun	女	woman	草	grass
辶	walk (quickly)	月	moon	小	small	火 灬	fire
豕	pig	舌	tongue	马	horse	竹 ⺮	bamboo
户	household	囗	enclosure	工	work	手 扌	hand
山	mountain	口	mouth			金 钅	metal

Exercise 6

Can you recognize the character according to the following description? Please give what you think is the meaning of each character. We have done one for you.

1 an eye with water   林 ＿＿＿＿＿＿

2 two trees next to each other 灾 ＿＿＿＿＿＿

3 bamboo with fur/hair underneath 囚 ＿＿＿＿＿＿

4 a person in an enclosure   从 _to follow_＿＿

5 fire under roof   泪 ＿＿＿＿＿＿

6 two people next to each other 笔 ＿＿＿＿＿＿

Exercise 7

Can you identify the meaning of the following characters with the help of their radicals? Again, we have done one for you. Refer back to the table of radicals to help you.

墙	to throw	吻	she
扔	wall	椅	warm
怕	sweat	暖	kiss
汗	fear	她	chair

14

Test yourself

1 What is the character which has a big square with a person in the middle?

2 What is the character which has a big square with a cross in the middle?

3 Which character has the character for 'field' as the top part of it?

4 When you write the 'person' radical 亻, on which side of the character should it go, the left or the right?

5 Is it true that a radical can appear on the left, right, top or bottom of a character?

6 Is it true that some radicals change the way they are written depending on the position they occupy in a character?

7 Is it true that all characters have a semantic radical, i.e. a radical that suggests the meaning?

3

....

Writing Chinese characters

In this unit you will learn:

- Some basic strokes
- Stroke order when writing characters
- A dozen more characters/radicals

Now it's your turn to write Chinese characters! Where do we begin? As you can imagine, there are some basic rules for writing Chinese characters which you need to master. This is important if you are to remember them accurately. Chinese characters should always be written the same way so that they become fixed in your memory. We have seen how most characters are made up of two or more components or structural parts, although some of these components such as 月 *yuè* (moon), 日 *rì* (sun) can stand by themselves, as we have mentioned earlier. Although the total number of characters is quite large, the number of components which go to make up these characters is very limited. These components are written with a number of basic strokes, which are illustrated as follows.

Stroke	Name	
﹀	*diǎn*	dot
—	*héng*	horizontal
∣	*shù*	vertical
ノ	*piě*	left-falling
ヽ	*nà*	right-falling
╱	*tí*	rising
ﻝﺍﻝﻝ	*gōu*	hook
ﬧﬧ	*zhé*	turning

These strokes are basically straight lines and were traditionally written in ink with a hair brush. The main directions are from top to bottom and from left to right. In the basic strokes that follow, the arrows show how the characters are written by indicating the direction each stroke takes.

The rules of stroke order in writing Chinese characters and character components are as follows.

Example	Stroke order	Rule
十	一 十	First horizontal, then vertical
人	丿 人	First left-falling, then right falling
三	一 二 三	From top to bottom
州	丶 丿 丬 州 丗 州	From left to right
月	丿 刀 月 月	First outside, then inside
四	丨 冂 冈 四 四	Finish inside, then close
小	丨 小 小	Middle, then the two sides

Let's go back to the table of radicals in Unit 2 and identify some of these basic strokes. Take the radical 工 for instance; it is made up of two horizontal and one vertical strokes. The rule is that you do the horizontal first, then the vertical and, working from top to bottom, you do the second horizontal last, so you write it like this:

工

NB: Horizontal strokes must always be written from left to right, viz 二.

小 is a symmetrical character so the middle stroke is done first, then the two sides, from left to right:

丿 小 小

土: first horizontal, then vertical and from top to bottom:

一 十 土

口 is an interesting case. When writing what amounts to a box, this part of the box ⌐ is done in one stroke, but this part ∟ is done as two strokes. This is all to do with what is and is not possible to do with a hair brush without dripping and what looks aesthetically pleasing. So, 口 is written:

丨 冂 口

It is still basically following the rules top to bottom, and from left to right.

日 is very similar in its stroke order but also follows the finish inside, then close rule:

丨 冂 日 日

月 follows the first outside, then inside rule:

丿 刀 月 月

Insight

It should be easy to understand that recognizing a character does not mean being able to write it. For some simple ones, i.e. those with fewer than three or four strokes, one's normal visual memory might be sufficient for you to recall the shape.

But what about characters with 10, 15, 20 or 25 strokes? There are many of these.

Physically copying a character many times in order to memorize how to write it is not an interesting or enjoyable task for most people. However, if you do want to memorize how to write characters, especially the complicated ones, copying them many times is said to be the most effective way, especially for long-term memory.

Exercise 1
Try working out the stroke order of the following eight characters and writing them in the gaps provided. (The number of gaps indicates the number of strokes required.) Writing small characters needs a lot of practice so we recommend that initially you use a separate sheet for this and subsequent exercises.

1 人 ___ 人
2 田 ___ ___ ___ ___ 田
3 大 ___ ___ 大
4 木 ___ ___ ___ 木
5 钅 ___ ___ ___ ___ 钅
6 山 ___ ___ 山
7 忄 ___ ___ 忄 or 心 ___ ___ ___ 心
8 言 ___ ___ ___ ___ ___ ___ 言

How did you get on? Check your answers in the **Key to the exercises**.

We're going to help you with the next ones to make sure you understand the stroke order correctly.

車 follows the basic rules, first horizontal, then vertical and from top to bottom, but there is an additional point to remember. When the vertical goes *through* the horizontal(s), it (the vertical) is done *last*:

一　厂　厅　亘　亘　車

By the way, 車 is a full character, the simplified character is 车 – much simpler, isn't it?

羊 also follows this rule:

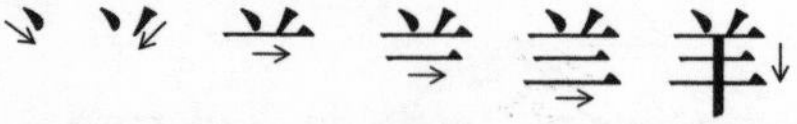

毛 and 舌 both start with the same stroke 丿, which was the second stroke in 羊 above:

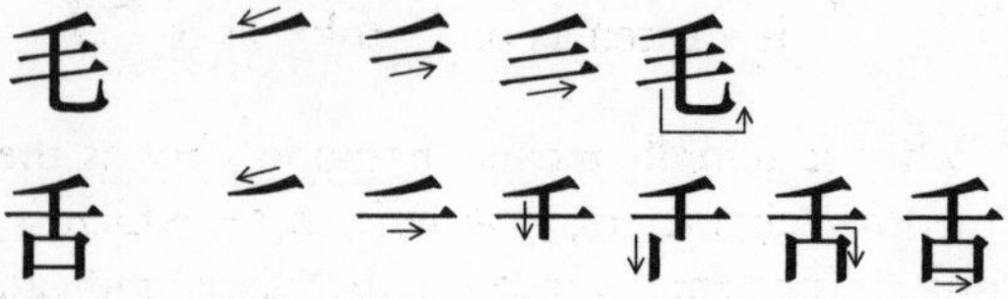

力 is written 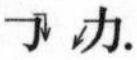.

女 is an interesting character. It originally came from the picture of a woman in a traditional, respectful position with her arms crossed over her stomach:

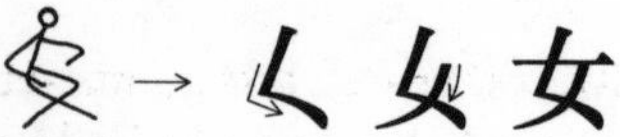

子, whose origins we looked at in Unit 1, is written as follows: 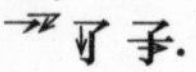. When used as a radical on the left-hand side, the last stroke is not horizontal but rising. Nevertheless, it moves in the same direction as the horizontal.

扌 has both these strokes in it:

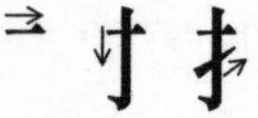

Have a go at the next six yourself. Each line represents one stroke. They're a little trickier than the ones you did before so we'll give you a little help now and again:

⺈ is in fact the radical 刀 *dāo* (knife) but is made much smaller and more stylized when it appears on the top of a character as it does here.

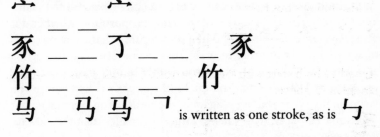

马 ＿ 弓 马 ㇇ is written as one stroke, as is ㇄

⺮ only appears as 竹 when it actually means 'bamboo', but as the meaning or radical for other characters, it is written ⺮, which is, fortunately, much simpler! The same is true for the 'grass' radical. It is 草 when written on its own and means 'grass' but is written as ⺿ (一 ⺿ ⺾) when it is acting as a radical.

You may need some help with the last ones: 火 can either be written 丶丿少火 (left to right rule), or 丶丿丿少火 (top to bottom rule). 灬 is, of course, written 丿丶丷灬.

辶 counts as *three* strokes: 丶辶辶 and is always written *last* no matter where it occurs in the character. This is probably because its last stroke finishes up right at the bottom of the character.

Exercise 2
Let's do some more practice on the basic strokes you have learned in this unit. In the table are five of these. Circle the stroke illustrated in the column on the left in each of the characters which follow. We have done one for you to show you what is required.

亅	小	材	少	尘	你
丶	心	言	家	米	兴
乛	打	河	冰	牲	跑
丿	力	长	火	户	石
一	大	舌	草	鱼	马

Each individual Chinese character occupies exactly the same amount of space, i.e. a square of the same proportions, whether it is imaginary or real. Chinese children start writing characters on pages of squared paper in order to maintain a better sense of proportion and balance. We have provided you with a sample page to practise on at the end of this unit. You might like to copy it first before you write on it so that you use it again in the future. You can make your own squared paper, with squares larger or smaller than the ones we have given you.

Insight

There are other ways of improving your writing of characters:

- Write the characters LARGE and small to appreciate the proportions and balance within each character (use different sizes of squared paper for this).
- Write them fast. Copy or write twenty different characters as fast as you can for, say, three minutes, and see how many you can write. Do it again after you've done some practice (e.g. two weeks later) and see if you can write more characters within the same length of time. The purpose of this exercise is to give you confidence and help you maintain the flow of your writing.

Exercise 3

Now that you have learned the basic rules about stroke order, how would you write the following characters?

Example: 水　丨　丿　才　水

1 月　—　—　—　月
2 牛　—　—　—　牛
3 户　—　—　—　户
4 穴　—　—　—　—　穴
5 当　—　—　—　—　—　当
6 米　—　—　—　—　—　米

Not only does each Chinese character occupy the same amount of space, whether it is a very easy character, e.g. 日, or a relatively complex one, e.g. 碗 *wǎn* (bowl), it must be in the right proportions.

22

This does not mean that you have to do any measuring of any kind, it is basically what is pleasing to the eye. Simple points to remember are that both 'halves' must be roughly level at the top and bottom, but there are notable exceptions to this. The radical 口 *kǒu* (mouth) (like a small enclosure 口) usually occurs on the left side of a character slightly lower than what is on the right-hand side, again for aesthetic purposes, e.g. 吃 *chī* (to eat) would look very ugly if it were written 吃 or even 吃.

Exercise 4

Look at the pairs of characters and circle the one in each pair which you think is better written.

A	a	B	b	C	c
大	大	好	好	月	月

D	d	E	e	F	f
火	火	马	马	水	水

Some characters **do** look similar. This may cause confusion and make it difficult for you to remember. However, it is important to spot the differences.

Can you see the difference(s) between the following pairs of characters? We have also provided you with the stroke order for each character.

人	person	ノ 人		入	to enter	ノ 入	
广	broad	丶 广		厂	factory	一 厂	
习	tricky	コ 习		习	to practise	コ ヲ 习	
己	self	フ コ 己		已	already	フ ヨ 已	
干	to do	一 二 干		于	at, in	一 二 于	
贝	shell	丨 冂 贝 贝		见	to see	丨 冂 贝 见	
东	east	一 七 左 东 东		车	vehicle	一 七 左 车	
石	stone	一 ア イ 石 石		后	rear; behind	一 厂 尸 斤 后 后	
我	I, me	ノ 二 于 手 我		找	to look for	一 十 扌 扌	
		我 我				扗 找 找	

Another rule about stroke order worth remembering is that the dot `in such characters as 我 and 找 always comes last. If it occurs inside an enclosure 口, however, it becomes the penultimate stroke, not the very last; e.g. in 国 *guó* (country) the stroke order is:

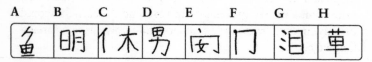

国 also illustrates a refinement to the basic rule, first horizontal then vertical. As you have seen, the vertical stroke is done *before* the last horizontal one, i.e. 干王 and not 三王. Remember that the vertical is done last when it *goes through* the last horizontal but not when it just touches it, so 三丰 but 干王.

Exercise 5

What is wrong with the following characters? (You have met them all in their correct form.)

A	B	C	D	E	F	G	H
鱼	明	亻木	男	安	门	泪	草

Now for some more radicals. In Unit 2, we introduced the concept of radicals. Do you remember what a radical is?

Exercise 6

What is a radical? Is it a:

a stroke in a character
b character component
c simple character?

We have seen how most Chinese characters are made up of two components – a radical and a phonetic. Radicals may be helpful in identifying the general area of meaning of the character but this is not always apparent. However, the radical will *always* help us find a particular character in a dictionary and hence its actual meaning (see Unit 10). For that reason, we need to learn as many of them as we can.

Exercise 7

What do these radicals mean? Can you infer their meanings from the translations given for each of the characters?

							Meaning
1	目:	眼 eye	盯 to stare	瞎 blind	眨 to blink	_____
2	犭:	狗 dog	狼 wolf	猫 cat	狐 fox	_____
3	饣:	饱 full up	饭 meal	饼 pancake	馅 stuffing	_____
4	刂:	刻 to carve	剁 to chop	割 to cut	刺 to pierce	_____
5	山:	峰 peak	岭 hill	崖 cliff	岗 hill	_____

....

Insight

You should not be surprised that many Chinese do not know what some of the components of characters mean. Similarly, many English speaking people do not necessarily know the root of a word or the origin of a prefix or suffix. This is largely due to the fact that when one learns one's mother tongue, one is usually too young to analyse the lexicon of one's native language. It has also become unfashionable to place too much emphasis on grammar. However, adult learners would usually find it a 'shortcut' to understanding words in a foreign language.

....

Exercise 8

Can you identify the radicals in the following characters? Write down the radical of each character in the space provided and say what the character might be to do with. Then check the **Key to the exercises** to see if you got them right.

Example:

Character	**Radical**	**Might have something to do with**
话	言(讠)	Speech

1 枫 _____ **2** 讽 _____ **3** 峰 _____

4 海 _____ **5** 晚 _____ **6** 煮 _____

7 资 _____ **8** 烧 _____ **9** 笔 _____

10 刻 _____

Exercise 9

Here are more radicals for you to remember (some have already appeared in this unit):

Radical	Pinyin	Meaning	Radical	Pinyin	Meaning
刂 (刀)	dāo	knife	石	shí	stone, mineral
饣 (食)	shí	food	口	kǒu	mouth
目	mù	eye	贝	bèi	shell
氵 (水)	shuǐ	water	见	jiàn	to see
牛 (牜)	niú	cattle	页	yè	page
彳		step with left foot	米	mǐ	rice (uncooked)

Try working out the stroke order for each of them and then check it in the **Key to the exercises.** We have deliberately put 贝 *bèi*, 见 *jiàn* and 页 *yè* together to show you how similar they are in one sense and how different they are in meaning. It may help you to think of 贝 *bèi* as being written with 'straight' legs, whereas 见 *jiàn* is written with one 'curly' one. 页 *yè* is just like 贝 *bèi* but it has ⌐ on top of it.

We have already noted that many radicals are to be found in the same position in any of the characters in which they occur. Look at the position of the various radicals in Exercises 7 and 8 and then do Exercise 10.

Exercise 10

Where does the radical normally go?

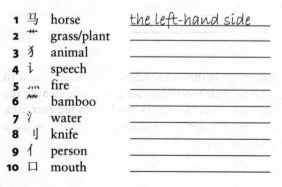

1	马	horse	the left-hand side
2	艹	grass/plant	
3	犭	animal	
4	讠	speech	
5	灬	fire	
6	𥫗	bamboo	
7	氵	water	
8	刂	knife	
9	亻	person	
10	口	mouth	

Exercise 11

Can you write the character according to the following description?
Please guess or give the meaning of the character if you can.

Description	Character	Meaning
1 Water (left) in an eye (right)	_____	_____
2 Two trees next to each other	_____	_____
3 Bamboo with fur/hair underneath	_____	_____
4 A person in an enclosure	_____	_____
5 Fire under roof	_____	_____
6 Small (top) earth (bottom)	_____	_____
7 Sun (top) above light (光)	_____	_____

Exercise 12

Group together all the characters that have the same radical.
Number the groups from **1** to **9** (there are nine groups altogether).
What does the radical in each group mean? (The answers will be in
the **Key to the exercises,** but not necessarily in the order you have
given them. When you have studied Unit 10, you should be able
to look up the characters you don't know in a Chinese–English
dictionary.)

泪 _1_	昨 ____	吃 ____	林 ____	推 ____	叮 ____
诗 ____	饭 ____	汗 _1_	时 ____	贵 ____	材 ____
杂 ____	货 ____	饺 ____	喝 ____	河 _1_	扣 ____
别 ____	刚 ____	贡 ____	词 ____	晚 ____	饿 ____
打 ____	吸 ____	说 ____	根 ____	刷 ____	订 ____

1 water	2 _____	3 _____
4 _____	5 _____	6 _____
7 _____	8 _____	9 _____

Exercise 13

How many strokes are there in these characters? They may be new to
you. Do not worry about their meanings. See if you can identify the
number of strokes in each character. Check the **Key to the exercises,**
where the strokes of these characters are illustrated (cf. how to use a
Chinese dictionary in Unit 10).

方　　山　　九　　足　　去　　气　　尺　　风

学写字 Learning to write

A Chinese child started to learn writing on his first day with his teacher. The teacher began by showing him how to write 一, the character for 'one'. The child said to himself: 'That was easy.' Then the teacher taught him to write 二, the character for 'two'. Seeing how easy it was to do 'two', the child became restless. Then he was shown how to write 三, the character for 'three'. Before he was asked to write it, he shouted in protest: 'I know how to write now!' The teacher said to him: 'You are a quick learner. So much for the lesson. Your homework for today is to write the character for "ten thousand".'

The character for ten thousand is 万 (full form 萬)

Test yourself

1 When writing the character 十 (ten), which stroke do you write first: the horizontal one or the vertical one?
2 What is the last stroke of the character 口 (mouth)?
3 How many strokes are there in 口?
4 How many strokes are there in 马 (horse)?
5 What is the first stroke of 山?
6 Which character is used by the Chinese to refer to the British flag: 水 木 米? (Think of the **form** of the Union Jack and then look at the three characters again – which one does it most resemble?)
7 人 (person) and 入 (enter) look similar but have different meanings. However, when you write them, do you follow the same stroke order, i.e. the left stroke preceding the right one or not?

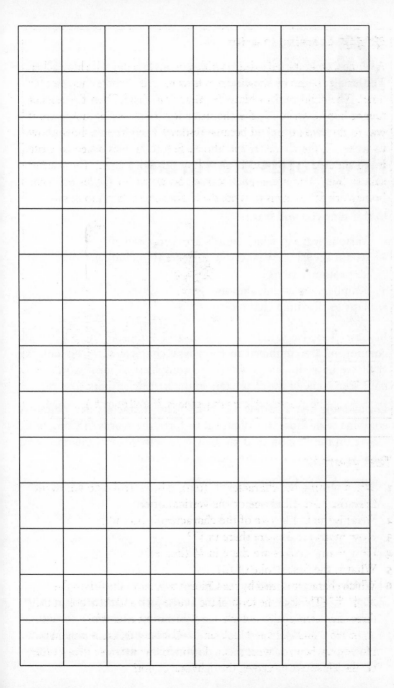

4

....

How words are formed

In this unit you will learn:

- Various ways in which words are composed
- About the Chinese language in general (including its pronunciation)
- Numbers, basic calculations, years in Chinese
- Tips for learning characters

In Units 1–3, we saw how radicals and a radical and a phonetic component are combined to form new characters. In this unit we shall see how single characters are combined to form words. You have seen some of the characters in the first three units.

Let us look first at a few examples. The characters in Column A combine with those in Column B to form the words in Column C. Cover up the English next to the Chinese words in Column C and see if you can work out the meanings for yourself.

Column A	Column B	Column C	
人 person	口 mouth	人口	population
入 to enter	口	入口	entrance
天 heaven/sky	子 child	天子	emperor
王 king	子	王子	prince
工 work	人 person	工人	worker
大 big	人	大人	adult; used in ancient times when addressing a person with status (and honour), e.g. a judge in the imperial court

小 small	人	小人 a dishonourable or small-minded person (*not* child/children)

These words are reasonably obvious. The next ones are not.

Exercise 1

What do you think the following mean? Check the **Key to the exercises** for the answers.

	Column A	Column B	Column C	Meaning
1	小 small	心 heart/mind	小心	_____
2	放 put down	心	放心	_____
3	瞎 blind	话 speech	瞎话	_____
4	笑 laugh	话	笑话	_____

Combining characters

There are different ways of combining single characters to form two-character words or even three- and four-character words. Here are some examples.

Noun + noun

电 electric(ity) + 话 speech = 电话   telephone
天 day, sky   + 气 air   = 天气   weather

NB: Both 天 and 气 are radicals in their own right.

Exercise 2

				Meaning
1	火 fire	车 vehicle	火车	_____
2	木 wood	工 worker	木工	_____
3	月 moon	票 ticket	月票	_____
4	电 electric(ity)	视 vision	电视	_____
5	电	车 vehicle	电车	_____
6	电	影 shadow	电影	_____
7	电	脑 brain	电脑	_____

风 wind + 水 water = 风水 wind and water?

风水 *fēngshuǐ* actually means **geomancy**. This early Chinese belief (and one which is still held by many Chinese throughout the world) holds that the spirits of land, water and wind play an active part in human affairs. Thus, the location and the direction in which a house or tomb faces, and even the position of the windows and furniture within the home, are of the utmost importance. They determine the fortunes of the family which occupies the house or of the relatives of the dead person. Tombs, for example, should face south with protecting hills behind them and a river or stream nearby so that good luck can flow to the family of the deceased.

The idea behind this is that people are part of the natural order; therefore, where they build their dwellings or graves must harmonize with the forces that exist in nature. Even some businesses (including non-Chinese ones) take 风水 into account when deciding on the height and exact location of their premises in an attempt to cut off the flow of good luck to their competitors. This is achieved by such measures as blocking out the sunlight to their offices and/or casting a shadow on them.

I told you the *fengshui* here was no good
我说过这儿的风水不好。

Adjective* + verb

好 good + 听 to listen = 好听 pleasant to listen to

难 hard, difficult + 吃 to eat = 难吃 awful (food)

*Adjectives in Chinese can also function as verbs, so 好 *hǎo* means 'to be good' as well as 'good'. Some people call such adjectives 'stative verbs' when they function in this way.

Exercise 3

Meaning

1 好 + 吃   好吃   _____

2 难 + 听   难听   _____

3 好 + 看 to look at   好看   _____

4 难 + 看   难看   _____

Adjective + noun

小 small + 学 study = 小学 primary school

公 public + 园 enclosure = 公园 park

Exercise 4

Meaning

1 大 big   学 study   大学   _____

2 小 small   费 fee   小费   _____

3 好 good   心 heart; mind   好心   _____

Exercise 5

公 public + 平 level = 公平   Does it mean:

    a to be fair; justice

    b scales

    c flat road?

明 bright + 天 day, sky = 明天   Does it mean:

    a yesterday

    b today

    c tomorrow?

Verb + verb

听 to listen + 说 to speak = 听说 to hear someone say

听 to listen + 懂 to understand = 听懂 to understand (through listening)

看 to look at + 懂 to understand = 看懂 to understand (through reading)

看 to look at + 见 to see = 看见 to have perceived by seeing (to have seen)

听 to listen + 见 to see = 听见 to have perceived by hearing (to have heard)

Verb + object

开 to start + 车 vehicle = 开车 to drive (a vehicle)
念 to read aloud + 书 book = 念书 to study

Exercise 6

What do you think the following verb–objects mean?

			Meaning
1	吃 to eat	饭 cooked rice	吃饭 _____
2	教 to teach	书 book	教书 _____
3	录 to record	音 sound	录音 _____
4	走 to walk	路 road	走路 _____
5	说 to speak	话 speech	说话 _____

Insight

As you can see from the last exercise, Chinese uses an object where you would not normally find one in English. Thus the English 'to eat' becomes 吃饭 'to eat cooked rice' in Chinese. This is because classical Chinese was monosyllabic (one-syllabled), whereas modern Chinese has become increasingly disyllabic (two-syllabled): the verb–object construction can be seen as conforming to the disyllabic trend. Using the 'fill-in' object also produces a more balanced sentence from the Chinese point of view. Of course, if the verb has a 'proper' object then the 'fill-in' object is discarded, e.g. 他 (he) 吃鱼 (eats fish) (where 'fish' is the object).

Duplicates for plurals

Do you remember what 人 means? Yes, it is 'person'. What then do you think 人人 means? It means 'everybody'. Logical, isn't it? When some words are repeated, the meaning is 'every' plus the noun in question. But not all nouns work in this way. Let us look at some more examples:

天: day   天天   every day
月: month   月月   every month
年: year   年年   every year
代: generation   代代   every generation

How to write the numbers 1 to 10

Let's try writing the numbers 1 to 10.

一	二*	三	四	五	六	七	八	九	十*
yī	èr	sān	sì	wǔ	liù	qī	bā	jiǔ	shí

* 二 and 十 are both radicals in their own right.

Stroke order: points to remember

a Remember that horizontal lines are done from left to right.
b From top to bottom. (三) 一 二 三
c Finish what is inside the box before closing the box.
(四) 丨 冂 冂 四 四
d Horizontal before vertical. (五) 一 丁 五 五
e Left falling before right falling. (六) 丶 亠 六 六
f 乙 counts as one stroke. (九) 丿 九 Some people write it as 乀 九.
The important thing is for *you* to always write it the same way.

Pronunciation and the Chinese script

This book is about the Chinese script, so we have decided not to spend a lot of time (and space) explaining the pronunciation to you. Please refer to *Complete Mandarin Chinese* and *Get started in Mandarin Chinese* if you want to learn to speak Chinese. In any case, spoken Chinese comes in many different dialects, the difference between many of them being greater than the difference between, say, English and German or Portuguese and Italian.

The Chinese script, however, remains the same for all of these dialects, the only difference being that since the People's Republic of China came into being in 1949, the government has simplified a number of common characters (well over 2,000) in an attempt to raise literacy levels in China. Until then, characters had remained virtually unchanged for about 2,000 years. Officially, Taiwan and Hong Kong do not use these simplified characters but some are used unofficially, for example when people write to one another and so on. Singapore has adopted the simplified system.

The dialect whose pronunciation system is adopted in this book, as well as in *Complete Mandarin Chinese* and *Get started in Mandarin Chinese*, is called *pǔtōnghuà* 普通话 'common speech'. It is sometimes referred to in the West as Modern Standard Chinese or Mandarin. More than 70% of Chinese people in the People's Republic of China speak some form of this dialect. It is also the official Chinese language or dialect in Taiwan and Singapore, where it is known as *guóyǔ* 国语 'national language' and *huáyǔ* 华语 'Chinese (old word) language' respectively.

A simple **Pronunciation guide** can be found at the back of the book.

How to write the numbers 11 to 99

Once you have learned the numbers 1 to 10, you will be able to read and write 11 to 99.

11 is $10 + 1 = $ 十一
12 is $10 + 2 = $ 十二
19 is $10 + 9 = $ 十九
20 is $2 \times 10 = $ 二十
30 is $3 \times 10 = $ 三十

41 is $4 \times 10 + 1 = $ 四十一
52 is $5 \times 10 + 2 = $ 五十二
87 is $8 \times 10 + 7 = $ 八十七
99 is $9 \times 10 + 9 = $ 九十九

Exercise 7
What numbers do the following characters represent?

a 四
b 八
c 五
d 七

e 九
f 六
g 十
h 十八

i 三十五
j 九十四
k 七十六
l 五十九

Exercise 8

Try writing out the following numbers in Chinese characters. Don't forget your stroke order rules. You can use the squared paper provided in Unit 3. This will help you to keep the characters the same size and with the correct spacing.

a 8　　**c** 7　　**e** 6　　**g** 4　　**i** 32　　**k** 65
b 10　**d** 5　　**f** 9　　**h** 21　**j** 87　　**l** 94

Numbers in lists

Although Arabic numbers are widely used in documents and newspaper articles, this traditional form of written numbers is still commonly used. In English, people use A, B, C, D for listing points. In Chinese, people tend to use 一二三四 for the same purpose. 第 in front of a number makes it into an ordinal (or ranking) number like first, ninth, etc. 第 has bamboo on top and the phonetic *di* underneath. It is written:

The equivalents to English first, second and third are 第(*dì*)一, 第二, and 第三 and not 第1, 第2, and 第3.

How to write the years

It is very easy to write the years in Chinese. Each figure is treated as a single number. Thus 1998 is said and written as 一九九八 with the character for year 年 *nián* written after it. 年 is written: ノ 仁 仁 仁 年.

Exercise 9

What are the following years?

a 一九一九　　**d** 一〇六六　　**g** 一四九二
b 一九九一　　**e** 一七八九　　**h** 一八四八
c 一九四五　　**f** 一九一四　　**i** 二〇一五

*Zero is the exception to the rule that Chinese characters are commonly used for writing numbers. The character for zero 零 is quite complicated so 〇 has been widely adopted instead.

Exercise 10

Write out the following years in Chinese characters (you don't need to write 年 after each one):

a 1321						f 1486				
b 1932						g 1937				
c 1876						h 1842				
d 1965						i 2037				
e 1949										

How to write the date

We have already come across the characters for sun and moon. They are 日 and 月. Understandably 日 and 月 also represent day and month respectively. Now, can you understand what the following dates are?

a 一月三日   **b** 十月八日   **c** 十二月二十五日

They are 3 January, 8 October and 25 December. This is really quite easy and completely logical but have you noticed that in Chinese, the month comes first? This is because the Chinese have a vertical rather than a linear concept of time and move from the general to the particular so the order is year, month, day, time of day (a.m./p.m.), hour, minute, which is the exact reverse of the English word order.

Insight

It should be noted that, although in most informal writing people use Arabic numbers for dates, in most formal writing dates are still written in characters, as in the examples we have just seen.

Learning tip: making your own flash cards

You can make your own flash cards as you work your way through the book. It would be a good idea to go back to Unit 1 and make them for Units 1–3 as well, as they contain a lot of useful, basic vocabulary.

A flash card normally consists of the character or characters on one side and the English and/or romanization on the other. A good size for your flash card is 3 cm.

Character   Reverse side

火   fire   *huǒ*
明   bright   *míng* or bright (sun + moon)

You could also put on the reverse side how the character is made up (see above); this might help you to remember it more easily.

Having made your flash cards (and of course you keep adding to them as you learn new characters), you work through them looking at the character side first and seeing how many of them you recognize. Check your answers with the English on the back. Put the ones you get right on one side and then work your way through the ones you got wrong, repeating the process until you recognize them all.

Having gone through your flash cards 'recognizing' the characters, do it the other way round. Look at the side with the English and the explanation as to how the character is made up and try writing out the character itself. This is, of course, much harder! Check your answer with the character on the other side. Adopt the same system as before, putting aside the ones you get right and repeating the ones you get wrong.

You will probably need to do this many, many times before you have mastered them and, as you add new flash cards to the old ones, there is always more to be done.

Find a handy sized box to keep your cards in, so that you can work on them on the bus, train or underground or in any spare moments you might have. You will be interested to know that even very young Chinese children learn their basic characters in this way. They used to have pictures on the front and characters on the back. The *pinyin* might be on the front or the back. The latest ones for learning characters also have English on the back!

Below are examples of the type of flash card you can make yourself.

A1	B1	C1	D1
难	钱	星期	电话
A2 *nán* difficult	**B2** *qián* money	**C2** *xīngqī* week	**D2** *diànhuà* telephone
E1 学习	**F1** 汉字	**G1** 生词	**H1** 卡片
E2 *xuéxí* study	**F2** *hànzì* Chinese character	**G2** *shēngcí* new words	**H2** *kǎpiàn* card

Are you ready to read and write some more dates? Try the following exercises.

Exercise 11

Can you recognize the following dates?

a 二月一日 d 四月十日 g 十一月二十六日
b 三月七日 e 六月二十日 h 十月十五日
c 五月九日 f 八月三十日 i 十二月三十一日

Exercise 12

Match the English months with their Chinese equivalents. We have done the first one for you.

a December   **b** April   **c** September
d June   **e** November   **f** May
g July   **h** October   **i** August

1 十一月   **2** 六月   **3** 八月
4 九月   **5** 七月   **6** 十二月
7 十月   **8** 四月   **9** 五月

Example: a December = 6 十二月

Exercise 13

Can you write out the following dates in Chinese characters?

a New Year's Day
(1 January)

b St George's Day
(23 April)

c American Independence
Day (4 July)

d Christmas Day
(25 December)

e Summer Solstice
(21 June)

Exercise 14

The cartoon depicts a man giving his wife flowers for International Women's Day. What is the date of this special day?

How to write the days of the week

All you need to know to write the characters for the days of the week are the two characters 星 *xīng* (star) and 期 *qī* (period) which, when combined together, form the word for 'week'; plus the numbers 1 to 6 and the characters for 'sun' 日 (*rì*) or 'day' 天 (*tiān*). 星 *xīng* is made up of the radical 日 *rì* (sun) and 生 *shēng* (to give birth).

We have given you the correct stroke order in the boxes:

期 *qī* is made up of the phonetic element 其 *qí* (its) and the radical 月 *yuè* (moon).

Practise writing the days of the week on your own. You have already met 日 *rì* (sun) and 天 *tiān* (day).

Exercise 15
Match the Chinese with their English equivalents.

a	星期三	**1**	Monday
b	星期六	**2**	Tuesday
c	星期一	**3**	Wednesday
d	星期日	**4**	Thursday
e	星期二	**5**	Friday
f	星期五	**6**	Saturday
g	星期四	**7**	Sunday

Exercise 16

Write the missing character in the space which gives you the correct day in answer to the following questions:

Example:

Which day comes two days before Thursday? 星期二

a On which day do Muslims go to the mosque? 星期____
b On which day do Christians go to church? 星期____
c Which day do Jewish people go to the synagogue? 星期____

....

Mini-test 1

You may find some of the exercises in the mini-test quite challenging. You may like to return to them after you have finished the book. Hopefully you will be amazed by the progress you have made.

Exercise 1

We have learned that in many characters there is one component which indicates the pronunciation. That component is called the **sound component**. Now that you have learned a number of meaning radicals, see if you can match the characters with their respective meaning in the following exercise. These characters sound very similar because they all share the same sound component 青 *qīng*. Put the appropriate number in the brackets. We have done one for you. (The one with the radical you don't recognize will be the character for 'cyanogen'!)

1 情 *qíng*	**a** to ask, to request
2 清 *qīng*	**b** dragonfly
3 鲭 *qīng*	**c** bright/sunny day
4 请 *qǐng*	**d** feeling
5 蜻 *qīng*	**e** cyanogen (a gas)
6 晴 *qíng*	**f** mackerel
7 氰 *qíng*	**g** clear

2 = **g**

Exercise 2

Identify the Chinese phrases and match up the correct number with the English translation. We have done one for you.

1 人民大会堂
2 人民币
3 人民日报
4 人民公园
5 人民广场

2 = e

a People's Square
b People's Park
c Great Hall of the People
d *People's Daily*
e Chinese currency

Exercise 3

What do you think the following words mean? Do they mean **a**, **b** or **c**? Circle what you think is the correct answer. (The dictionary definition of each individual character is provided.)

1 生日   **a** sunrise   **b** birthday   **c** early morning
生 to be born; raw   日 sun; day

2 早安   **a** dawn   **b** settlement   **c** good morning
早 early   安 peace; put in place

3 日历   **a** diary   **b** calendar   **c** rainbow
日 sun; day   历 history

Exercise 4

Try and fill in the missing characters in the captions above the picture. We have tried to help you by giving you the basic meaning of each of the characters you will need to use. 午 occurs more than once.

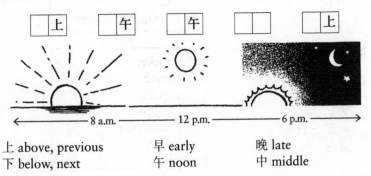

上 above, previous   早 early   晚 late
下 below, next   午 noon   中 middle

Exercise 5

Guess what the caption below the cartoon means. You have already met the word 公平 earlier in this chapter. Can you find it again? (不 *bù* means 'not' and is put in front of all verbs except 有 *yǒu* (to have) to negate them.)

不公平

Which side of the shop window is menswear?

Exercise 6

Some characters occur as part of many different words. 中 (middle) and 火 (fire) are good examples of this. What do you think the following words mean? For each word, choose what you think is the correct translation from the box on the right.

a

中学
中国
中心
中午

| noon |
| centre |
| Chinese language |
| Chinese newspaper |
| China |
| secondary school |

b

火腿 (leg)
火山
火车
火箭 (arrow)
火花

| rocket |
| torch |
| spark |
| volcano |
| fireworks |
| train |
| ham |

Exercise 7

What is the radical for the following words? (2) means you should try to write the two versions of the radical.

a	mouth	**b**	rain	**c**	fire (2)
d	page	**e**	wind	**f**	knife (2)
g	rice	**h**	child	**i**	metal (2)
j	eye	**k**	horse	**l**	speech (2)
m	big	**n**	field	**o**	heart (2)
p	woman	**q**	mountain	**r**	step with left foot
s	door	**t**	to walk		

Finally, here are 14 more radicals for you to learn – you've come across half of them already:

Radical	Pinyin	Meaning	Radical	Pinyin	Meaning
八 or 丷	*bā*	eight	纟	*sī*	silk
天	*tiān*	day, heaven	衤/衣	*yī*	clothing
王	*wáng*	king	冫(冰)	*bīng*	ice
门	*mén*	door	禾	*hé*	grain, plant
风	*fēng*	wind	穴	*xué*	cave, hole
虫	*chóng*	insect	气	*qì*	air
广	*guǎng*	covering, roof	犭	*quǎn*	(wild) animal, dog

The stroke order for these is fairly straightforward:

八 丿 八 or 丷

天 一 二 天 天

王 一 二 王 王

门 丶 门 门

风 丿 几 风 风

虫　丨冂口中虫虫

广　丶一广

纟　乡纟纟

衤　丶ラ衤衤衤

衣　丶一ナ右衣衣

冫　丶冫

冰　丶冫丬冰冰冰

禾　一二千禾禾

穴　丶冖宀穴穴

气　丿一气气气

犭　丿犭犭

Note the difference between 禾 grain and 天 day. In 禾 the first
stroke is sloping ノ but it is horizontal 一 in 天.

5

Signs (1)

In this unit you will learn:

- Practical signs in e.g. hotels and restaurants
- Some common Western names in Chinese characters
- Country names in Chinese characters
- How to tell the time in Chinese

From this unit on, we are going to take you through your business trip to China. You are attending a conference in Beijing, and will do some sightseeing and shopping.

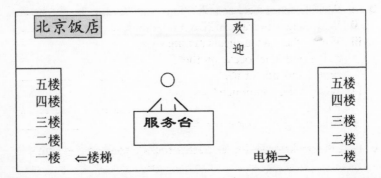

生词 *Shēngcí* **New words**

The radical for each character is shown in brackets after it.

北京	*Běijīng*	Beijing
北	north	(⼁or ヒ)
京	capital	(亠)
饭店	*fàndiàn*	hotel; restaurant
饭	rice, meal	(饣)
店	shop	(广)
楼梯	*lóutī*	stairs
楼	building	(木)
梯	stairs	(木)
服务台	*fúwùtái*	reception
服务	to serve; service	(月 力)
台	platform; station	(口)
服务员	*fúwùyuán*	attendant
员	person	(口)
欢迎	*huānyíng*	to welcome
欢	joyfully	(又)
迎	to greet	(辶)

Exercise 1

a Identify the new radicals (i.e. ones you *haven't* met in Units 1–4) in the new words in the list and write them in the spaces provided.

___ ___

		Radical	Meaning
b	**i** What is the radical of 饭?	_____	_____
	ii What is the radical of 楼?	_____	_____
	iii What other two radicals (acting as the phonetic) occur on the right-hand side of 楼?	_____	_____
	iv What is the component below 口 in 员?	_____	_____
	v Give the stroke order for 迎. ___ ___ ___ ___ ___ ___ ___

c Give the stroke order for 梯 (rather tricky). You had 弟 in Unit 4.

木 ___ ___ ___ ___ ___ ___ ___ ___ (梯)

弟 *dì* means younger brother and is normally reduplicated i.e. 弟弟 as are 爸爸* *bàba* (dad), 妈妈 *māma* (mum), 姐姐 *jiějie* (elder sister) and 哥哥 *gēge* (elder brother), 妹妹 *mèimei* (younger sister).

d What is the radical for 妈妈? For 姐姐? For 哥哥? For 妹妹?

*父 *fù* is another new radical, meaning 'father' or elderly male person.

Exercise 2

What do you think the following Chinese words mean?

电梯   (bottom right corner on the hotel floor
        map above)
店员   (cf. 服务员)
服务楼
电台   (cf. 服务台)

Insight

The first floor in China is the ground floor in Britain, and the second floor in China is the first floor in Britain, and so on. America uses the same system as China.

Exercise 3

Having settled down in your hotel room, you decide to have some lunch. There are two restaurants in the hotel. Follow the sign 餐厅 (canteen or restaurant) and you see a 服务员 giving you directions. You have a choice of two restaurants, Cantonese (*Guǎngdōng*) or Sichuan. Which is which?

By the way, there is a sign on the left-hand column in the picture below (禁止吸烟) asking you not to do something. (Check Unit 2 to see what the radicals 口 and 火 mean. This will help you.) Is it asking you:

i not to take photographs   **iii** not to dump litter
ii not to smoke   **iv** not to enter

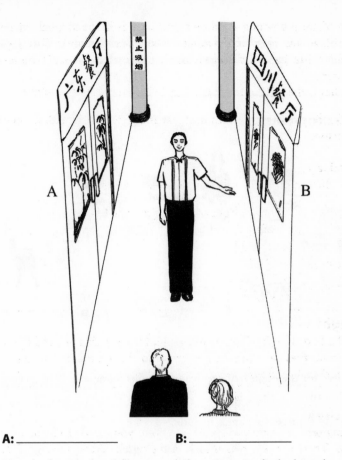

A: _____   B: _____

Now look at the hotel floor map below. Can you find where the toilets are? Do you remember 男 *nán* and 女 *nǚ* introduced in Unit 2? Yes, they are 'man' and 'woman'. The Chinese for 'toilet' is 厕所 *cèsuǒ*.

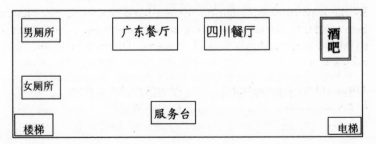

There is one more new word on the map. It is in the top right-hand corner. You will come across it again soon. But look at the radical of the first character and you may have an idea what it is.

At the conference

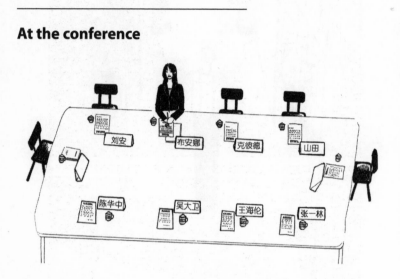

It is time for the conference to begin. If your name is 王海伦, where will you sit?

Common Chinese surnames include:

张	王	李	赵	刘	陈	林	吴	郭	郑
Zhāng	*Wáng*	*Lǐ*	*Zhào*	*Liú*	*Chén*	*Lín*	*Wú*	*Guō*	*Zhèng*

Note: They do not all appear in the illustration, but 王海伦 will sit third from the left at the bottom of the picture.

Insight

These ten surnames are among the most common in China. While Zhao, Liu, Wu are purely for people's names and place names, Zhang, Wang, Li, Lin, Guo, Chen and Zheng have other meanings. As you already know, 林 *lín* is 'forest' and 王 *wáng* is 'king'. 张 *zhāng* means 'to stretch', and 李 *lǐ* is 'plum'.

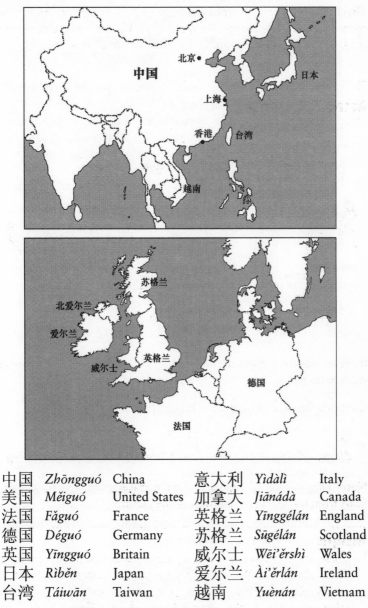

中国	*Zhōngguó*	China	意大利	*Yìdàlì*	Italy
美国	*Měiguó*	United States	加拿大	*Jiānádà*	Canada
法国	*Fǎguó*	France	英格兰	*Yīnggélán*	England
德国	*Déguó*	Germany	苏格兰	*Sūgélán*	Scotland
英国	*Yīngguó*	Britain	威尔士	*Wēi'ěrshì*	Wales
日本	*Rìběn*	Japan	爱尔兰	*Ài'ěrlán*	Ireland
台湾	*Táiwān*	Taiwan	越南	*Yuènán*	Vietnam

香港　*Xiānggǎng* Hong Kong
北爱尔兰　*Běi'ài'ěrlán* Northern Ireland

生词 *Shēngcí*　　　New words

中	centre, middle	中国: the Middle Kingdom
法	law, rule	*Fǎ* sounds similar to the first syllable of 'France'
英	hero	*Yīng* sounds similar to the first syllable of 'England'
美	beautiful	*Měi* sounds similar to the second syllable of 'America' (the second syllable (i.e. *me*) of 'America' is stressed, hence more prominent)
德	virtue	*Dé* sounds similar to the first syllable of 'Deutschland'
香	fragrant	
港	harbour	

Exercise 4

Match the participants with their nationalities.

王海伦 英国	山田 日本	李明芳 法国	张一林 中国	吴大卫 美国	刘安 香港

1 Who is from Japan?

2 Where is 吴大卫 from?

3 Is Ms Wang from China?

4 Which country does Ms Li represent?

5 Is there anybody from Germany?

6 What is the surname of the Hong Kong participant?

Translation of English names

English names, or any foreign names for that matter, are translated into Chinese mainly according to what they sound like to the Chinese ear. Chinese characters which sound similar are used to represent the sound. The table that follows gives some examples of this.

Another way of creating a Chinese name is to choose a character for one's surname and one or two characters for one's given name. (In Chinese the surname or family name should come first, followed by one's given name and finally one's title, when used.) The characters in one's Chinese name should ideally be close, in terms of sound or meaning, to the non-Chinese name. The surname, of course, should come first, and the first name should be second to make it resemble a Chinese name.

Some common English names and their Chinese translations

Given names	Pinyin	Characters	Given names	Pinyin	Characters
John	*Yuēhàn*	约翰	Clare	*Kèlái'ěr*	克莱尔
David	*Dàwèi*	大卫	Karen	*Kǎilún*	凯伦
Colin	*Kǎolín*	考林	Helen	*Hǎilún*	海伦
Peter	*Bǐdé*	彼德	Anna	*Ānnà*	安娜
Robert	*Luóbótè*	罗伯特	Jane	*Jiǎn*	简
Mark	*Mǎkè*	马克	Lisa	*Lìshā*	丽莎
Surnames			**Surnames**		
Smith	*Shǐmìsī*	史密斯	Brown	*Bùlǎng*	布朗
Clinton	*Kèlíndùn*	克林顿	Green	*Gélín*	格林
Blair	*Bùlái'ěr*	布莱尔	Black	*Bùláikè*	布莱克

Exercise 5

Your Chinese friends have told you what their names mean. Can you write down their names in characters?

A 'My given name is Guo'an. "Guo" means "country" and "an" means "peace".' ___ ___

B 'Mum and Dad gave me the name of "big bright". They obviously hoped that I would be a star.' ___ ___

C 'My given name is Yinglin. "Ying" means "hero" while "lin" means "forest".' ___ ___

D 'Because I was born in Beijing, I am called Jingsheng, literally meaning "capital-born".' ___ ___

How to write the time

In Unit 4, we learned the Chinese characters for dates. Now let's look at time. Look at the pictures of the clocks and the Chinese characters below, and work out what characters mean *hour* (as on the clock), *minute*, *a quarter* (of an hour) and *half* (of an hour). Circle one example of each (character) in the times given in the Chinese below.

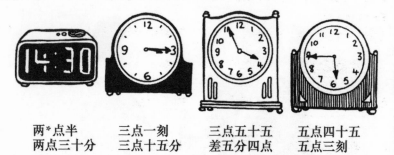

两*点半   三点一刻   三点五十五   五点四十五
两点三十分   三点十五分   差五分四点   五点三刻

*Note that 两 *liǎng* (two) is used where there are two of a kind, instead of 二 *èr*.

The five new words used for expressing time are:

点 *diǎn* o'clock	分 *fēn* minute	刻 *kè* a quarter
半 *bàn* half	差 *chà* lack; missing	

Did you get them right? Let's take a closer look at these characters and see if we can find a way of remembering them.

QV

点 has the fire radical underneath. It also means to 'light a fire'. When it got dark, people would light a candle, hence the character has to do with time. The classical or complicated character for 点 is 點, which has 'dark' or 'black' on the left side. 分 means 'to divide', as expressed by a 刀 (knife), which is the bottom radical of 分. The character then means 'division', and was later used to represent a division of time. It is also used to represent the smallest unit of Chinese money. The right-hand side of 刻 is also a knife. It is called a 'vertical knife' or a 'standing knife'. 刻 means 'to carve or engrave', and as a noun it refers to a short period of time. 半, meaning 'half', is straightforward: a line cutting through the middle breaking it into two equal parts. 差 is made up of the radical for sheep 羊 *yáng* (slanted here) and the phonetic element 工 *gōng*. No help here for pronunciation, unfortunately.

Insight

Although Arabic numerals are widely used in China when expressing numbers, traditional characters like 八、九、十, are still used everywhere, especially in a formal context, such as the dates in a document as well as the times on a sign indicating the opening hours of a shop.

Exercise 6

What are the opening hours of the following places?

a	中国银行	九点 ---- 十七点
b	森林餐厅	早七点 ---- 晚十一点
c	邮电局	八点半 ---- 十九点
d	办公室	上午八点 --- 十二点 下午两点 --- 六点

Exercise 7

Now for some quick revision. What are the radicals of these characters? (Try not to refer to the explanations given earlier.)

a 分 ___   d 钟 (钟 *zhōng* means 'clock')
b 刻 ___   e 差 ___
c 半 ___

Exercise 8

Write in characters the time on each of the clocks:

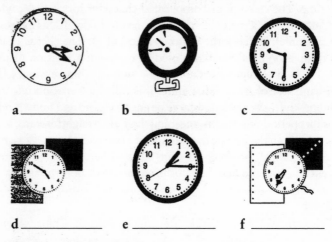

a _____ b _____ c _____

d _____ e _____ f _____

Back to the conference

Saturday's and Sunday's itinerary for the conference participants is shown below.

日程表

第三天星期六

早上	七点半	--	八点	早饭	
上午	八点半	--	十一点半	开会	
中午	十二点	--	一点	午饭	上海餐厅
下午	一点半	--	四点	开会	
晚上	六点	--	七点半	晚饭	四川餐厅
	八点			电影	《日出》

第四天星期日

| 上午 | 参观北海公园 |
| 下午 | 参观清华大学 |

生词　　*Shēngcí*　　New words*

*. . . but actually you've seen more than half of them already.

日程表	*rìchéngbiǎo*	itinerary
程		journey
表		form; table; watch

第	*dì*	ordinal number prefix (see Unit 4)
早上	*zǎoshang*	early morning
上午	*shàngwǔ*	morning
中午	*zhōngwǔ*	noon
下午	*xiàwǔ*	afternoon
晚上	*wǎnshang*	evening
上海	*Shànghǎi*	Shanghai
开会	*kāi huì*	hold a meeting
开		to open, to start
会		meeting
参观	*cānguān*	to visit
日出	*rìchū*	sunrise
出		to go/come out
北海	*běihǎi*	north sea
北		north (see 北京 at the beginning of this unit)
海		sea
公园	*gōngyuán*	park (see Unit 4)

Exercise 9

What are the radicals for:

程; 表; 第; 早; 上; 中; 午; 下; 晚; 开; 会; 参; 观; 海; 公; 园

Exercise 10

Answer the following questions based on the itinerary we have just seen, first in English, then in characters where possible.

1 Where will you have lunch on Saturday?
2 When is lunch?
3 What will you do on Saturday evening at 8 p.m.?
4 When will the afternoon session start?
5 When are you having meetings on Saturday?
6 What are you doing on Sunday morning?
7 What kind of institution are you visiting on Sunday afternoon?

Exercise 11

It's 10 p.m. after the film show. You might feel like going to the 酒吧 (bar) for a drink before going to bed.

啤酒	(beer)
葡萄酒	(wine)
可口可乐	(Coca-Cola)
咖啡	(coffee)
茶	(tea)
矿泉水	(mineral water)

Look at the menu and identify the radicals in the characters. Do you think that the radicals make sense?

Exercise 12

The English and Chinese on the following two signs have got confused. Can you put them right? What should the order of the English words be in **a**?

a

Now write out the correct sequence for the Chinese characters in **b**.

b

Exercise 13

Here is the layout of a hotel lobby. Can you identify what the various signs mean?

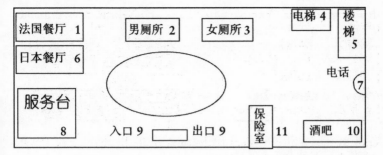

Give the English equivalent after each number as indicated in the picture. One has already been done for you.

1 _____
2 _____
3 _____
4 _____
5 _____
6 _____
7 _____
8 _____
9 _____
10 _____
11 _deposit boxes_ _____

Let's revise the radicals that have occurred for the first time in this unit and learn some more new ones.

Radical	Pinyin	Meaning	Radical	Pinyin	Meaning
亠		above	玉	yù	jade
又	yòu	again, also	寸	cùn	inch
父	fù	father	疒	bìng	illness
足	zú	foot	鸟	niǎo	bird (long-tailed)
走	zǒu	to go, walk	巾	jīn	towel, napkin
舟	zhōu	boat	立	lì	to stand
戈	gē	spear	礻		omen; to express
阝 on LHS		mound	酉	yǒu	spirit made from ripe millet; tenth of Twelve Earthly Branches*
阝 on RHS		town, region			
攵		to tap, rap			
方	fāng	square			

*If you would like to know a little more about the Earthly Branches and the Heavenly Stems and their connection with the Chinese zodiac, refer to *Complete Mandarin Chinese*.

Points to remember

- When we say X minutes past the hour, we use 分 for 'minute'. However, when we say X minutes, we tend to say X 分钟. So we say 十点十分 but 十分钟.

- Although 上 and 下 appear to be nearly mirror/reversed images of each other, in fact they are not. While the short stroke in 上 is flat or horizontal, the last stroke in 下, the short stroke in the middle on the right-hand side, goes downwards.

- Although these days most writing is done from left to right, i.e. horizontal, you still see writing done from top to bottom, such as on public signs (e.g. 禁止吸烟 in the picture).

- You may notice that in Chinese 'morning' and 'afternoon' are 上午 and 下午, where 上 and 下 mean 'top/up' and 'below/down' respectively. 午 is 'noon'. There are many time expressions where the Chinese use 上 and 下 for the sequence. For example, 上一次 ('the last time'), 下个月 ('the next month'). It seems that the Chinese tend to perceive a time line as vertical: the past has come down all the way from the top and times goes down into the future.

Test yourself

1 What is the position of a Chinese surname in a full name?
   a It comes first   **b** It comes last   **c** Its position does not matter
2 一楼 in China is: **a** the first floor *or* **b** the ground floor in Britain?

6

Signs (2)

In this unit you will learn:

- More signs to help you get around
- Directions
- More words for places in Chinese

Revision exercise

Let's revise the radicals we have already learnt by recognizing them in some of the characters we have met so far. Group together all the characters that have the same radical (there are ten radicals in all). List all ten radicals below the box. Try and remember what each character means. You can check your answers in the **Key to the exercises**.

出 ___	下 ___	华 ___	梯 ___	北 ___	河 ___
湖 ___	园 ___	二 ___	上 ___	法 ___	东 ___
南 ___	楼 ___	香 ___	晚 _1_	弟 ___	分 ___
半 ___	三 ___	共 ___	海 ___	李 ___	十 ___
星 _1_	公 ___	汽 ___	国 ___	程 ___	中 ___

1 _日 sun_   2 _____   3 _____   4 _____   5 _____

6 _____   7 _____   8 _____   9 _____   10 _____

Time for some sightseeing

The conference is over. You decide to go to 香山公园, a beautiful park in the western suburbs of Beijing. You can travel either by 出租汽车 (taxi) or by 公共汽车 (bus). You may notice that both 'taxi' and 'bus' contain the word 汽车, which in fact means 'vehicle'.

QUICK VOCAB

出租汽车	(*chūzūqìchē*) taxi
出租	for rent or hire
– 出	out
– 租	rent; to rent
汽车	vehicle
– 汽	steam, gas
– 车	vehicle
公共汽车	(*gōnggòngqìchē*) bus
公共	public
– 公	public
– 共	common; to share

Now would you be able to follow the sign and go to the right place to get on a bus or a taxi?

| 出租汽车站 | 公共汽车站 | (开往香山) → |

Insight

The word for 'bus' is different depending on where you are. It is 公共汽车, or 汽车 for short, in the People's Republic of China. It is called 公车 (still a public vehicle as the characters suggest) in Taiwan. In Hong Kong, where Cantonese is spoken, a bus is called '*bāshì*', which is in fact how the locals pronounce 'bus'. The characters for '*bāshì*' are 巴士, which do not mean anything but represent the sound only. 巴士, however, is being increasingly used in China, especially in Guangdong Province (Canton).

At the park entrance, you see a map of the park. You should be able to identify the places on the map. If you are not sure of any of them, just examine the radical(s) of the words carefully.

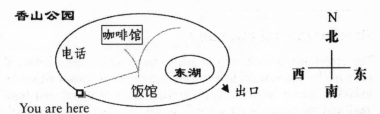

You are here

Exercise 1

Check the signposts and answer the following questions (which your friend who has no knowledge of Chinese characters might ask you).

1 In which part of the park is the lake?
2 Which way will you turn if you want to have some hot drinks?
3 Where will you find a telephone kiosk?
4 If you decide to have a meal, which way should you turn?
5 Where is the exit?

Direction words

Now let's learn the direction words. These words are not only often found in place names, but also in people's names.

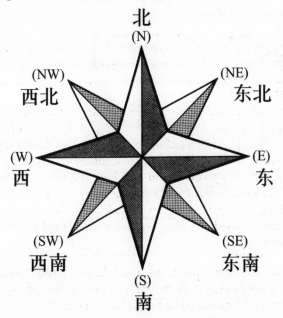

Do you remember the following words – 东南、东北、西南、西北?

Yes, they are SE, NE, SW and NW in English, i.e. the reverse of the Chinese word order. Note the use of、between the items. This is known as a pause mark and is used in a list after each item where we would use a comma in English. A comma is reserved for longer pauses in Chinese.

The following Chinese cities/provinces all have direction words in them:

北京、西安、南京、河北、河南、山东、山西、广东、广西、湖南、湖北、海南、西藏

QUICK VOCAB

河	*hé*	river
广	*guǎng*	broad
湖	*hú*	lake
海	*hǎi*	sea
藏	*zàng*	the Zang (Tibetan) nationality

Insight

Now you know the Chinese characters for China: 中国, the Middle Kingdom. The Chinese regarded China as lying at the centre of the world, hence the name.

When listing the cardinal points we say north, south, east, west, whereas the Chinese say 东南西北 (E, S, W, N) or 东西南北 (E, W, S, N) for the four directions. They also use the phrase 东西南北中 to refer to the whole country. There is a TV programme called 东西南北中 which introduces places of interest from all over China.

东方 and 西方 are 'the East' and 'the West'.

Exercise 2

See how many places you can recognize on the map below.

Place names in China

河北、河南 The Yellow River divides the two provinces. One is north of the river, hence 河北, and the other south of the river, hence 河南.

山东、山西 Taihang Mountain is between Shangdong and Shanxi Provinces, hence the names 山东, east of the mountain(s) and 山西 west of the mountain(s).

湖南、湖北 Hubei and Hunan Provinces are north and south of 洞庭湖 Dongting Lake, one of the biggest lakes in China.

Exercise 3

Do you know where these places are?

1 中东
2 地中海
3 南美
4 北海 (near the UK)

Exercise 4

Match the road signs with their correct *pinyin* equivalents:

a

c

b

1 Zhongshan Bei Lu
2 Ren He Lu
3 Ping Hai Lu

Exercise 5

a On the photo of
  Zhongshan Bei Lu
  (Ex. 4c), in which direction
  will you be going if you go
  left?
b If you go right?
c In which city was the
  photo on the right taken?

Exercise 6

Match the requests in Column A with the characters in Column B.
Where should someone go when:

A		B	
a	s/he wants a drink	i	电话
b	s/he wants to go to the toilet	ii	饭馆
c	s/he wants to have a meal	iii	酒吧
d	s/he wants to make a telephone call	iv	厕所

Exercise 7

Match up the English notice with its correct Chinese equivalent. We have done one for you. Two of the characters are in full-form characters. Can you spot which?

a Exit **b** Toilets **c** No smoking
d Taxi **e** Duty-Free **f** Flower Shop
g British Education Exhibition

e = 2

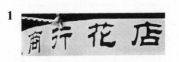

Exercise 8

What should you do or not do when you see the following signs? Sometimes you may only recognize one character in the sign but believe it or not, you can still do the exercise!

Exercise 9

Can you spot the mistakes in these phrases? Circle the incorrect character and write its correct form. Look at the cartoon below if you are not sure.

a 请勿昭相   **b** 小心解电
c 请勿吸咽   **d** 请勿随地灶痰

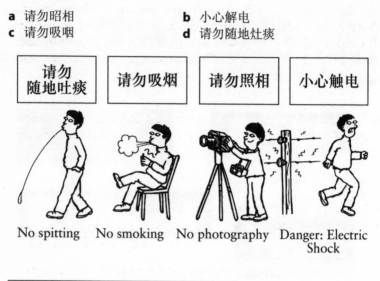

| 请勿
随地吐痰 | 请勿吸烟 | 请勿照相 | 小心触电 |

No spitting   No smoking   No photography   Danger: Electric Shock

---

Formation of new characters

In Unit 2, we looked at various ways of creating new characters: radical plus radical, radical plus phonetic. Here are two much less common methods but ones which are of great interest. In the first group, one component is the radical and the other component serves a double function, representing both the meaning and the sound:

女 + 取 (*qǔ*) to obtain   → 娶 (*qǔ*) to marry (as of a man taking a woman into his family)

女 + 家 (*jiā*) family, home → 嫁 (*jià*) to marry (as of a woman being taken into her husband's family)

These two examples also show us the patriarchal nature of traditional Chinese society. Women married into their husbands' families and it was customary for the women to live with their in-laws, not for the husbands to live with theirs. It was only men from very poor families, who could not afford to pay a bride price, who moved into their wives' homes. This was considered to be very shameful and in such cases the children of the marriage would take their mother's family name. In this context, it is interesting to note that the character for 'treacherous' or 'traitor' was 姦 (*jiān*); it also meant 'adultery'. It is now written 奸, but nevertheless the fact remains that the radical is 女. The character for 'slave' 奴 (*nú*) also has a female radical.

In the second group, two separate characters (not always radicals) are put together to form new characters. The meaning of the new character is directly related to both of the original characters. Do you remember 不 *bù* (not) in 不公平?

不 + 正 *zhèng* (straight)   = 歪 *wāi* (crooked)
不 + 好 *hǎo* (good)   = 孬 *nāo* (bad)
不 + 用 *yòng* (use)   = 甭 *béng* (don't)
不 + 口 *kǒu* (mouth)   = 否 *fǒu* (deny; or not)
                               (as in 是否 'whether or not')

The pronunciation of such characters is interesting. The pronunciation of 歪 *wāi* bears no resemblance to *bù* or *zhèng* but sounds suitably crooked. The other three have taken on some of the characteristics of their 'parents'!

Exercise 10
Which radical is missing? (We have put the English translation of each word in brackets to help you.)

a 娄上 (upstairs)   **b** 艮行 (bank)
c 酉吧 (bar)   **d** 反店 (restaurant)

Exercise 11
Fill in each of the blanks with **one** of these characters: 员、车、酒、泉. Again, we have put the English translation in brackets to help you.

a 火__站 (train station)   **b** 葡萄 ___ (wine)
c 矿__水 (mineral water)   **d** 服务 ___ (attendant)

Exercise 12

Match the signs with their correct translation:

禁止停车   Beijing University

北京大学   Bank of France

法国银行   Shanghai-bound train

开往上海   No parking

Exercise 13

Complete the following passage by filling in the missing characters from the list provided. Each character may be used once only.

我 (wǒ I, me) 星期 **1** ＿＿ 去 (qù to go) 北 **2** ＿＿ 开 **3** ＿＿。
我们 (wǒmen, we) 下午两 **4** ＿＿ 到 (dào to) 四点 **5** ＿＿ 开会。
晚 **6** ＿＿ 八点三 **7** ＿＿ 去看 (kàn to see) 电 **8** ＿＿。明天
9 ＿＿ 期天我们去参 **10** ＿＿ 北海公 **11** ＿＿。

| 京 | 刻 | 影 | 观 | 园 | 上 | 点 | 会 | 星 | 半 | 六 |

Exercise 14

Put the following Chinese sentences into the correct order as indicated in the passage in English:

I eat my breakfast at 6.30 a.m. I *like* (喜欢 xǐhuān) drinking coffee. I don't eat rice for breakfast. I go *to work* (上班 shàng bān) at 7.15. I drive to work.

1 我早饭不吃米饭。
2 我开车上班。
3 我早上六点半吃早饭。
4 我喜欢喝咖啡。
5 我七点一刻去上班。

The correct order is: ＿ ＿ ＿ ＿ ＿.

Exercise 15

Translate the following passage into English:

我在南京饭店住了四天。第一天服务员说：'欢迎你来南京饭店住。' 我住三楼。第二天上午我去玄武湖公园参观，

下午去中山陵，晚上去看电影。第三、第四天在南京大学开会。第三天中午在广东餐厅吃饭，第四天中午在上海餐厅吃饭，**都很**好吃。第五天早上七点吃早饭。七点三刻坐出租汽车去火车站，坐八点十分的*火车**回**北京。

在	*zài*	at
住	*zhù*	to live/stay
了	*le*	grammatical particle indicating the completion of an action
你	*nǐ*	you (singular)
来	*lái*	to come
玄武湖	*Xuánwǔ Hú*	name of a lake in Nanjing
中山陵	*Zhōngshānlíng*	(see picture below)
都	*dōu*	both, all
很	*hěn*	very
回	*huí*	to return

QUICK VOCAB

*的 *de* This character is required for grammatical purposes (see *Get started in Mandarin Chinese*, Unit 3). For the purposes of this exercise you can ignore it; the meaning of the phrase should still be clear.

中山陵 Dr Sun Yatsen's Mausoleum

Test yourself

1 What character has two mountains, one on top of the other?

2 In Exercise 1, you learned 出口 meaning 'exit'. 出口 also has another meaning. Does it mean 'import' or 'export'?

3 What is the meaning of the character which occurs at the beginning of each of the following words?
公共汽车 'bus'; 公园 'park'; 公路 'road'; 公安局 'police'

4 You will see 公用电话 signs in China for public telephones. 公 means 'public', 电话 means 'telephone'. What does 用 mean? Is it:
   a public   **b** use   *or*   **c** network?

5 What is the Chinese for northeast?
   a 东北   *or*   **b** 北东

6 Which of the two sets of characters below is the way the Chinese say the four directions of the compass?
   a 北南东西   *or*   **b** 东西南北

7 北京 'Beijing' is the north capital. 南京 'Nanjing' is the south capital. We know that 東 is the traditional character for 东. Now do 東京, the characters the Japanese use for Tokyo, mean:
   a the east capital   *or*   **b** the west capital?

7

Signs (3)

In this unit you will learn:

- More characters in advertisements
- Some characters used in menus
- How to fill in simple forms

Let's do some more work on signs. The ones in this exercise are much more difficult than those in Unit 6, but even if you only recognize one or two characters in each sign you should be able to match it with its English equivalent from the box below. We have done one for you. The English translations all come from real life!

Exercise 1

a 国际、香港到达

b 吸烟室

c 行李检查

d 凭票入内

e 欢迎使用太平洋信用卡

f 办手续

g 旅游投诉电话

h 南京中国国际旅行社

i 黄线范围内禁止停放车辆

j 本区唯一书店

1 No More Book Shop Ahead

2 Baggage Inspection

3 No Parking Within the Yellow Lines

4 Smoking Lounges
5 Tourists' Complaint Hotline
6 International, Hong Kong Arrivals
7 Welcome to use the Pacific Credit Card
8 No Entry Without Ticket
9 Check-In
10 Nanjing China International Travel Service

b = 4

A selection of Chinese notices, all of which appear in Exercise 1, follows. One of them is in full-form characters. Can you spot which?

i

国际、香港到达

ii

旅游投诉电话

杭州市旅游质监所:5171292
杭州市园文局:7025793

iv

本區唯一書店

iii

行李检查

You now have a few days off before you fly home via Shanghai where you have some business to attend to. You decide you'd like to do some shopping. To save time, you take a taxi from the hotel. As you get into the front, you notice a sign* on the front passenger's window: 前排客座只准坐婦女、兒童. (婦, a woman holding a broom, is the full form of the simplified character 妇, and 兒 is the full form of the simplified character 儿 which means 'child/son' and is also a radical.) The driver points to the sign and indicates that you should sit in the back. Do you know why? (Men are not allowed in the front seats of taxis, in case they hit the driver over the head or try to rob him – it's thought women are less likely to do this!)

*This sign was seen in Shenzhen near Hong Kong.

You arrive at a large shopping mall. Look at the floor plan and then do the exercise which follows it. Your knowledge of radicals will come in handy here!

A 中国银行		D 山东饭店	E 邮电局
B 电器商店			H 肯德基
C 电影院		F 食品商店	G 新潮衣店

生词 *Shēngcí* **New words**

局	*jú*	office
器	*qì*	appliance
品	*pǐn*	product
商	*shāng*	business, commerce
店	*diàn*	shop

Exercise 2

1 Is **D** a cinema or a restaurant?
2 Do you go to **B** or **E** to post a letter?
3 Where do you go to buy clothes?
4 Which is the bank?
5 Would you buy a Cornetto or Kentucky Fried Chicken at **H**?
6 Where do you go to buy food?

Exercise 3

You are surprised to see how many brand names commonly found in the West you can see in the shopping mall. In the next exercise there are five brand names in Chinese characters. Give the English equivalent for each of them. Which is the odd one out? (We've given you some of the *pinyin* to help you.)

a *kē ní kǎ*
柯尼卡

b *kěn dé jī*
肯德基

c *bèi kè píjiǔ*
贝克啤酒

d *chūn lán*
春兰冰箱

e *kě ài duō*
可爱多

If you're finding this difficult, the photos below may assist you:

a

c

d

b

e

Exercise 4

A Chinese friend with a car is driving you back to your hotel. You come to a large intersection. Your friend is a wonderful man but tends to be a little stingy. Will he take the left fork (**a**) or the right (**b**)? (Notice the characters 公 in (**a**) and 费 in (**b**), both of which you met in Unit 4.)

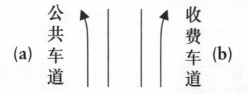

Which one would normally be the better road?

Exercise 5

You get back pretty late, happy but tired, and decide to have a relaxing morning the next day with a late breakfast in your room. Unfortunately you've only been left the Chinese Breakfast Room Service card (below and overleaf) to hang on your door. You decide to give it a go. You work out that there are four different types of breakfast. Can you list them in English in the order they appear on the card?

贵宾姓名：_____

人　　数：_____

签　　名：_____

房间号码：_____

日　　期：_____

所需服务时间
□6：00 – 6：30 □6：30 – 7：00 □7：00 – 7：30 □7：30 – 8：00
□8：00 – 8：30 □8：30 – 9：00 □9：00 – 9：30 □9：30 – 10：00

a　**国际特式早餐**　　　　　　　　　　　　　80.00
　　各式果汁任选
　　□ 橙汁　　　　　　□ 蜜瓜汁　　　　□ 西瓜汁
　　扒芝士火腿多士
　　蛋花热麦片
　　新鲜提子苹果碟
　　饮料任选
　　□ 咖啡　　　　　　□ 茶

b 美式早餐   **78.00**

各式冰冻果汁任选
☐ 橙汁   ☐ 西柚汁   ☐ 菠萝汁
☐ 提子汁   ☐ 苹果汁   ☐ 蕃茄汁
农场鲜鸡蛋两只任选
☐ 炒   ☐ 煎双面蛋   ☐ 煎
☐ 波   ☐ 焓…… ……分钟
配
☐ 火腿   ☐ 烟肉   ☐ 香肠
特式包点两件
☐ 牛角包   ☐ 丹麦包   ☐ 多士
☐ 麦菲   ☐ 早餐包
新鲜水果伴酸奶
饮料任选
☐ 咖啡   ☐ 茶

c 欧陆式早餐   **59.00**

各式冰冻果汁任选
☐ 橙汁   ☐ 西柚汁   ☐ 菠萝汁
☐ 提子汁   ☐ 苹果汁   ☐ 蕃茄汁
特式包点两件
☐ 牛角包   ☐ 丹麦包   ☐ 多士
☐ 麦菲   ☐ 早餐包
选择其中一款
☐ 酸奶   ☐ 鲜果碟
饮料任选
☐ 咖啡   ☐ 茶

d 中式早餐   **63.00**

瑶柱、白果白粥
腩汁蒸肠粉
选择其中一款
☐ 炸油条   ☐ 叉烧包
中国茶

所有价格另加 15% 服务费

e What do the last two characters in each category mean?

f What is the one character that is common to all four categories in addition to 早餐?

g What does it mean (have a guess)?

h In the first five lines at the top of the card, you are asked to give some of your details including your name, number of guests, signature, room number and date. Would you be able to fill them in? (Today is 10 August.)

Exercise 6

You decide to go for the second category at ¥78.00. You realize that where there is a line of characters and then a series of boxes underneath you are probably expected to tick *one* of the boxes. You do this and hang the notice outside your door. The next morning your breakfast tray has on it apple juice, two over easy (done on both sides) fried eggs, served with ham, two slices of toast, fresh fruit yoghurt and a pot of coffee.

a Which boxes did you tick? (Go back and tick what you ordered.)

b What did you get without having to tick a box for it?

c Write it out in Chinese characters too.

d Identify the characters for service charge and write them out.

e How much does the service charge add to your bill?

Exercise 7

After a leisurely breakfast you decide to fill in the guest questionnaire. In the Food and Beverage section you tick 'good' for the Cantonese restaurant, 'very good' for the Sichuan restaurant and 'fair' for Room Service (the eggs were hard). Which columns do you tick?

	很好	好	一般	差
广东餐厅				
四川餐厅				
送餐服务				

Exercise 8

You also need to reconfirm your flight to Shanghai. On the form which follows, the English translations have been deleted. Can you put them back in? (You will have to best guess a few of them!) Oh, and fill out the form in Chinese, where you can.

Flight Confirmation Request		**航班确认申请**
姓 _____	名 _____	房号 _____
航空公司 _____	离开日期 _____	护照号码 _____
航班号 _____	起飞时间 _____	
目的地 _____		
备注 _____		
日期 _____	客人签名 _____	接收人 _____

Exercise 9

You now have to book a hotel in Shanghai. A friend has given you two lists of possibles, one in Chinese and one in English, but they are not in the same order. Can you match the two? (Bear in mind that the English translations, although authentic, are not always very accurate.)

1 城市酒店（上海）
2 上海日航饭店
3 上海扬子江大酒店
4 花园饭店（上海）
5 广东国际大酒店
6 上海国际贵都大饭店

a Garden Hotel Shanghai
b Hotel Equatorial
c Hotel Nikko Shanghai
d GITIC Plaza Hotel
e City Hotel Shanghai
f Yangtze New World Hotel

One of the hotels is not even in Shanghai! Your friend must have made a mistake. Which one is it?

1

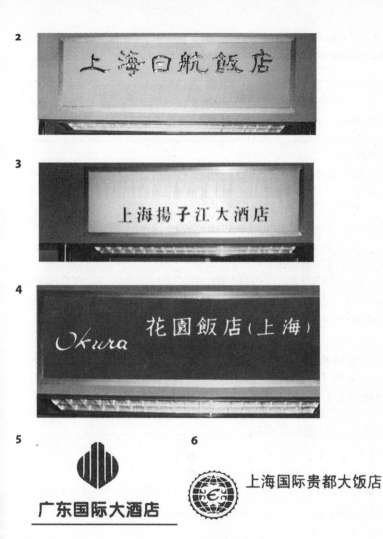

2 上海日航飯店

3 上海揚子江大酒店

4 Okura 花園飯店（上海）

5 广东国际大酒店

6 上海国际贵都大饭店

Exercise 10

Look at the hotel names in Chinese more closely:

  i Do they all use the same word for hotel?
 ii Which three hotels put the character for 'big' in front of the word 'hotel'?
iii In 花園飯店, are the characters written in full form or simplified characters?

iv Where does the word Shanghai appear in the Chinese version of Hotel Nikko Shanghai?

v In which other hotel signs does the same thing happen?

vi For which two hotels does the word 'Shanghai' appear in brackets?

vii For which two hotels does the word 'Shanghai' appear in the Chinese but not in the English?

Insight

As big cities in China compete to appear 'international', English translations have been added to many public signs and posters, resulting in confusion if not fun. Here are some examples.

http://www.squidoo.com/funnychinesesigns

http://www.tripntale.com/trip/411/china-funny-chinese-signs-translated-to-english

http://lichao.net/eblog/funny-english-translations-to-some-signs-in-china-200805140.html

The point is: it still pays to learn to read Chinese characters.

Exercise 11

You have just remembered you need to send off an urgent letter to a business acquaintance who is on holiday without a phone or fax. You write the letter quickly and find an envelope on your desk.

a What do you think 航空 means? (cf. radical 舟)

b Identify the two characters for postage stamp(s) by circling them. (贴邮票处 means 'stick stamp place'. cf. 'post office' in Exercise 2.)

c You know 姓名 means 'name' and 地址 means 'address'. What do you think 及 means?

d 收 in 收件人 means to 'receive'. What do you think 寄 in 寄件人 means?

e Write down the characters for 'sender' and 'recipient'.

Test yourself

1 In Exercise 1, 黄线 means yellow line. What is the radical for the character 线 'line'? (You might need to refer back to Exercise 7 in Mini-test 1.)

2 What is the meaning of the character shared by these three words?
电器商店   食品商店   新潮衣店

3 In Unit 2, we learned two characters, each of which consists of three of the same 'single' character: 森 and 焱. In this unit, we see another character with such a structure. Do you remember what it is?

4 What is the meaning of the character shared by these words (as seen in Exercises 5 and 7)?
早餐   四川餐厅   送餐服务

5 In Exercise 7, the category 差 means 'poor'. Do you remember that we used 差 when we talked about time in Unit 5? What did it mean there?

6 In the English word 'international', the word 'nation' is embedded in it. In the Chinese word 'international' 国际 (Exercise 1), which character stands for 'nation'?

7 In Exercise 11, the word 地址 means 'address'. What is the meaning of the radical for both characters?

8

Entertainment

In this unit you will learn:

- How to read characters on tickets
- How to read posters about shows and exhibitions
- About characters used on currency
- Measurements in Chinese characters
- More Chinese place names in characters

After a busy day, you decide to see a Chinese film. At the local cinema, you see that three films are on show that evening.

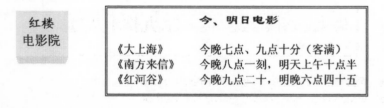

红楼
电影院

今、明日电影

《大上海》　　今晚七点、九点十分（客满）
《南方来信》　今晚八点一刻，明天上午十点半
《红河谷》　　今晚九点二十，明晚六点四十五

QV　红　*hóng*　red　　　　谷　*gǔ*　valley

Exercise 1

Please answer the questions in Chinese.

a What is the name of the cinema?
b Which show is sold out?

c It's nearly 8 o'clock. What is the next film available?

d What films are showing tomorrow?

Seating in Chinese cinemas, theatres, etc.

All the even seat numbers are grouped together on one side and all the uneven ones on the other. Only seat numbers 2 and 1 are next to each other sequentially. This means that when you go into a Chinese cinema for example, you need to check whether your seat numbers are even or odd. If they are even you will need to follow the sign for 双号 *shuānghào* seats and if odd the signs for 单号 *dānhào* seats. It is obviously important to understand the way the seating is organized if ever you are buying seats yourself and to know that 楼上 *lóushàng* means 'upstairs' and 楼下 *lóuxià* 'downstairs'.

Exercise 2

You are going to see a show and your ticket looks like this:

红楼电影院   电影票

六月二十日   楼上
晚七点四十五分   九排十八号

---

1 Will you be sitting upstairs or downstairs?

2 Which entrance do you go to? (i.e. odd or even numbers)

3 What time will the show start?

4 What is the date of the show?

Exercise 3

You are staying at 北京饭店. Look at the bus stop board.

(Here is another example where characters are written vertically.)

Now decide first which direction and then how many stops you should take before you:

a get to the People's Park.
b get to the Children's Amusement Park.
c get to the Tiandi (Heaven and Earth) Market.
d get to the Oriental (East) Hospital.

Exercise 4
Look at the following posters and answer the questions below. (The questions can refer to any of the posters.)

A 英国教育展	B 英文图书展销会
时间：六月九日 - 六月十七日	时间：五月七日至五月十八日
地点：北京大学	地点：星星书店（学院路1号）
免费入场	欢迎光临

C	D
法国印象派画展	日本电器产品展销会
时间：五月十四号 - 五月二十日	时间：六月二十四日至七月九日
地点：中国美术馆	地点：北京展览馆
票价：20元	票价：10元

1 Where is the British Education Exhibition taking place?
2 How much does it cost to go the French Impressionist Exhibition?
3 What is on sale at the Japanese Fair?
4 Books in which language are being exhibited at the Star Bookshop?
5 How many days is the French Impressionist Exhibition on for?
6 Which two exhibitions are free?
7 Which exhibition is on for the longest?

Exercise 5

A fairly standard form can be seen below. Try and work out what information you are being asked for. (We have added letters for ease of reference.)

a 姓名：	**b** 中文：	**c** 英文：
d 性别：	**e** 出生年月： 　　年　月　日	
f 现住址：		
g 电话：	**h** 工作单位：	

Insight

The measurements used in China are different from those used in the UK. The following is a table of measurements:

1 尺 (*chǐ*)	= 1.094 英尺 (*yīngchǐ*) foot
1 英尺	= 0.305 米 (*mǐ*) metre
1 米	= 1.094 码 (*mǎ*) yard
1 码	= 0.914 米
1 公里 (*gōnglǐ*)	= 0.621 英里 (*yīnglǐ*) mile
1 英里	= 1.609 公里 kilometre
1 斤* (*jīn*)	= 1.102 磅 (*bàng*) pound
1 磅	= 0.454 公斤 kilogram

*斤 is a radical in its own right.

Exercise 6

Prepare a note to give to a taxi driver, telling him where you want to go. You can start the note with 我要去 which means 'I want to go to', although this is not essential. For example: 'I want to go to Number 12 Peace Road' – 我要去和平路12号. You will find all the characters you need on the bus stop in Exercise 3.

a 8 West Lake Road
b The Oriental Hotel
c The Children's Amusement Park
d The People's Park

Exercise 7

Give the stroke order of the following characters, and put the radical in the brackets after each one.

饭   — — — — — — — — ( )
楼   — — — — — — — — — — — — — — ( )
河   — — — — — — — — — ( )
院   — — — — — — — — — — ( )
场   — — — — — — ( )

You are now on your way to the airport. First of all you have to pay the airport tax.

How much is it? Yes, ¥50, but have you noticed that 50 is not written as 五十 but as 伍拾? This is because numbers on tickets, receipts, coupons and bank notes, on forms in banks and post offices, etc. are written differently from the (simple) ones you learned in Unit 4. This is to prevent forgeries or misunderstandings. (It would be easy, for instance, to make 一 into 三.)

Here are the two lists of numbers for you to compare:

Ordinary numbers 一 二 三 四 五 六 七 八 九 十
'Complex' numbers 壹 贰 叁 肆 伍 陆 柒 捌 玖 拾

Three examples of bank notes, which all use the 'complex' numbers, follow. There are ten 角 (*jiǎo*) in one 圆 (*yuán*) (which is also written in the full form; 元 (*yuán*) is the simplified form used in daily life).

Exercise 8

Your business in 上海 is finished and you are flying from 上海 to pick up your flight in 香港 (Hong Kong). Here is your boarding card (登机牌).

Air China		登机牌	中国民航	
航班号	日期	时间	目的地	登机门
5359	六月七日	九点四十	香港	后门

a What are the Chinese characters for 'destination'?
b What is the date and time of your flight?
c Which door are you told to take, the front door or the rear one?

You are given the menu for the meal you will be served during the flight. It is shown in both simplified and full characters. The full-character version was the original and is on the right.

轻膳	輕膳
上海 -- 香港	上海 -- 香港
青瓜沙律	青瓜沙律
*	*
韩式牛骨排	韓式牛骨排
白饭	白飯
中式鲜蔬	中式鮮蔬
或	或
咖哩烩鸡	咖哩燴雞
野米饭	野米飯
*	*
鲜果	鮮菓
*	*
面包、牛油	麵包、牛油
*	*
红茶、日本绿茶、中国茶	紅茶、日本綠茶、中國茶
咖啡	咖啡

Exercise 9

Answer the following questions based on the menu above. (You may find it easier to circle some of the answers on the menu rather than writing them out or translating them into English.)

a What do the characters 香港 mean?
b Is rice served with the meal?
c Is beef (牛) or lamb (羊) on the menu?
d You have two choices of main meal, which are joined by the character for 'or'. Which is it?
e What is the dessert? (Go back and check what the character for 'fresh' is, Unit 2, Exercise 2.)
f Which hot drinks can you choose from after the meal? (红 *hóng* = red; 绿 *lǜ* = green)

You are now on your flight back to London (伦敦). The services offered by the cabin crew are shown on the card (which is authentic):

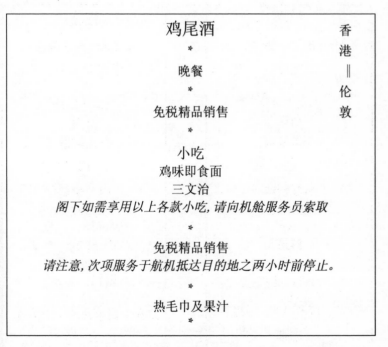

鸡尾酒

*

晚餐

*

免税精品销售

*

小吃
鸡味即食面
三文治
阁下如需享用以上各款小吃, 请向机舱服务员索取

*

免税精品销售
请注意, 次项服务于航机抵达目的地之两小时前停止。

*

热毛巾及果汁

*

香
港
‖
伦
敦

Insight

You probably know that 红 (*hóng*), the colour red, is auspicious for the Chinese. You see a lot of red at a Chinese wedding: the bride's dress, the flowers, the tablecloths, the carpet, etc. In Chinese the national flag is the red flag 红旗 (*hóngqí*). At Chinese New Year, adults are supposed to give children 红包 (*hóngbāo*), a little red bag containing some money.

Exercise 10

Answer the following questions (some good guesswork is required!):

a How many times is 'duty free' (see Unit 6, Exercise 7) mentioned?
b How many hours before landing does in-flight shopping stop?
c Circle the characters for 'attendant'.
d What do you think 小吃 are?
e Which comes first on the menu, snacks or dinner?
f What is a 三文治 (*sānwénzhì*)? (Say the whole word aloud and you should be able to guess it correctly.)
g What do you get with your wake-up towel – an apple, fruit juice or coffee?

Insight

In the People's Republic of China there are four municipal cities (Beijing, Shanghai, Tianjin and Chongqing), 22 provinces (excluding Taiwan), five autonomous regions (including Tibet) and two special administrative regions (Hong Kong and Macao).

Each has a single character as its short form. Here are some examples:

北京	*Běijīng*	京	四川	*Sìchuān*	川
上海	*Shànghǎi*	沪 *hù*	广东	*Guǎngdōng*	粤 *yuè*
天津	*Tiānjīn*	津	香港	*Xiānggǎng*	港
山东	*Shāndōng*	鲁 *lǔ*	青海	*Qīnghǎi*	青
湖南	*Húnán*	湘 *xiāng*	西藏	*Xīzàng*	藏

This is used in a number of situations. Some of the railway lines and motorways are named after the two cities or provinces connected by them. For example, 京沪线 (线 *xiàn* 'rail line'), 京津公路 (公路 *gōnglù* 'highway'), 青藏公路 etc. The regional styles of opera are thus termed 京剧 (剧 *jù* drama), 沪剧, 川剧. Types of cuisine are also called 川菜, 粤菜 etc.

Points to remember

- The English word for 'pound' can refer to the unit of money or to the unit of weight. The Chinese characters for the two meanings are 磅 and 镑. You should be able to tell which is which from their radicals.

- The Chinese still widely use 斤 (*jīn*), half a kilogram, for weight in daily life just as some market sellers in Britain still use the pound as their measure of weight.

- The Chinese words 楼上 and 楼下 mean 'upstairs' and 'downstairs' respectively. You will notice that the word order in Chinese is the opposite/reverse of the English word order.

- In English, two of the most common words in place names are 'road' and 'street'. Similarly, the two words in Chinese are 路 (*lù*) and 街 (*jiē*). (You will notice the 足 'foot' radical in 路 and 彳 'steps' radical in 街.) 路 is the more general word, whereas 街 tends to refer to a road in a residential area or a high street with shops along it, etc. Another explanation has it that 路 is used for east–west roads, while 街 is used for north–south roads. There are, however, many 'exceptions' to the rule.

- On the tube or metro in Beijing, for instance, the train stations are indicated as the train moves along. So your knowledge of Chinese characters will help you to follow your journey.

9

....

The weather

In this unit you will learn:

- Some common wishes
- Some set phrases and proverbs involving numbers
- How to read the weather forecast in newspapers
- How to write simple postcards or messages
- About Chinese calligraphy

This unit will provide you with general information on the weather and how to write notes and postcards in Chinese. It will also include a section on calligraphy and the different styles of writing Chinese characters which have always been highly prized by the Chinese.

You have been back in Britain for six months now and feel very proud of the postcard you have just written to your Chinese friend for his birthday: you feel your writing has made real progress!

大明,
　　你好!
　　我回英国已经六个月了, 工作常常很忙, 可是我很高兴。
我很想你! 下个月是你的生日, 祝你:
　　生日快乐! 身体健康! 工作愉快! 万事如意!
　　　　　　　　　　你的朋友
　　　　　　　　　　海伦
　　　　　　　　　　九月十八日

生词	*Shēngcí*	**New words**
回	*huí*	return
已经	*yǐjīng*	already
工作	*gōngzuò*	(to) work
常常	*chángcháng*	often
忙	*máng*	busy
可是	*kěshì*	but
高兴	*gāoxìng*	happy
想	*xiǎng*	to miss (somebody); to think (of)
生日	*shēngrì*	birthday
祝	*zhù*	to wish
快乐	*kuàilè*	happy, pleasant
身体	*shēntǐ*	body, health
健康	*jiànkāng*	healthy
万事	*wànshì*	10,000 matters
如意	*rúyì*	as one wishes
朋友	*péngyou*	friend

The Chinese often finish their letters by using phrases like:

Literal meaning

祝你: Wish you . . .

走运!	Walk lucky	Good luck!
生日快乐!	Birthday happy	Happy birthday!
一路平安!	All the way peace	Bon voyage!
身体健康!	Body healthy	Good health!
工作愉快!	Work happy	Happiness in your work!
万事如意!	10,000 things as wish	May everything turn out exactly as you would wish it!

Common greetings at festivals are:

祝你: Wish you . . .

新年快乐!	新 new	年 year		Happy New Year!
春节快乐!	春 spring	节 festival		Happy (Chinese) New Year!
情人节快乐!	情 affection	情 人 lover		Happy Valentine's Day!
复活节快乐!	复 again	活 living		Happy Easter!
圣诞节快乐	圣 holy	诞 birth		Happy Christmas!

Insight

The Chinese seem to have a passion for numbers. Many idioms have numbers in them. 万事如意 is one of them. 万 is a particularly favoured word in Chinese culture. Unlike in English, where 10,000 means 'ten thousand', the Chinese has a term 万 for it, and it represented and still represents a very large number. While in English one may wish someone (or a cause) a long life by saying 'Long live XX', the Chinese equivalent is to wish someone or something to live 万岁 *wàn suì* '10,000 years'. Therefore, 万岁 was used to address or greet emperors. Understandably, it was also used for Mao Zedong, the late Chinese leader. His supporters used to wave his little red book and shout: '毛主席万岁、万万岁!' '*Máo zhǔxí* wàn suì、wàn wàn suì!*'

*主席 *zhǔxí* chairman

Here are some other commonly used idioms with numbers in them:

	Literal meaning
一心一意	one heart, one mind
三心二意	three hearts and two minds
一心二用	one heart, two uses
一国两制	one country, two systems
三言两语	three words and two speeches
七上八下	seven ups and eight downs
百年大计	100 years big plan
千山万水	1,000 mountains and 10,000 waters
千家万户	1,000 families and 10,000 household(s)
千言万语	1,000 words and 10,000 speeches

Exercise 1

Here are the 'proper' translations for some of the idioms above, but they are not in the same order. Can you match them up?

not giving undivided attention to something
to be in two minds
whole-hearted(ness); with undivided attention
to be in a state of anxiety and nervousness

(of speech) brief
(covering) a vast area of land
every family and household
(there is) a great deal to express
a project of vital and far-reaching importance

Exercise 2

We feel we must give you the chance to practise your weather vocabulary! Here is the weather forecast 天气预报 *tiānqì yùbào* for tomorrow in a Chinese newspaper.

<人民日报>	四月二十七日 星期六

天气预报

今天白天晴	今天晚上阴, 有小雨
风向: 南风	风向: 西北
风力: 一、二级	风力: 四、五级
最高气温20°C	最低气温8°C

1 When will the weather be fine today?
2 What direction will the wind be coming from
   a during the day? **b** during the night?
3 Will the wind be stronger in the evening or during the day?
4 When will it rain?
5 What is tomorrow's date?

报上说今天不会下雨

But the paper said it wouldn't rain today

Exercise 3

Read the following postcards and answer the questions after them. (The questions can refer to any of the postcards.)

小王:

你好!
我们的会谈很成功,我认识了很多新朋友。这里的饭菜都很好吃。
我现在住在和平饭店,

祝你春节快乐!

你的朋友 李和平
九八年一月十五日

美:

你好!南京天气很不好,天天下雨。我很想你。
祝你情人节快乐!爱你!

大海
二月六日

小明:

你好!
北京真好。每天天气都很好,不冷不热。
昨天我去了人民大会堂。我明天去西安。

祝你圣诞节快乐!

你的朋友   马天民
二〇〇〇年十二月七号

---

1 Which hotel was Li Heping (李和平) staying in?
2 What was the food like at Li Heping's hotel?
3 Which city was Ma Tianmin (马天民) staying in?
4 Where did he go yesterday?
5 Where was the weather good?
6 Where did it rain?
7 Why was Dahai (大海) writing to Mei?
8 Where is Ma Tianmin going tomorrow?
9 When did Li Heping write to Xiao Wang?

Insight

Traditionally, Chinese writing was done from right to left and from top to bottom. This tradition has been largely kept in Hong Kong and Taiwan, where newspaper articles as well as books are still mostly printed vertically. The following is an illustration.

平衡集

英語

九七年前，人們對回歸祖國以後有很大假設或者看法，到了今天發覺並不一一實現，例如九七年之後此地人們不再覺得要學好英語。

近十年間，香港的大學生英語水準下降是人所周知的事，法律學生自不例外，於是早幾年前有些人覺得香港法庭變成中文世界的日子即將來臨，英語好不好也不打緊了，法庭遲早全用中文聆訊，政治正確最重要。那知道過了九七，不止香港人仍在學英語，國內的人更多在學英語，原來，根據統計數字，此刻中國國內在學英語的學生比在美國說英語的美國人還要多。

Calligraphy

Even today, the art of calligraphy (the writing of Chinese characters as an art form) is highly regarded in China and many educated Chinese will hang scrolls of characters, beautifully mounted, on their walls, just as we would hang a picture by, say, Turner or Picasso. Calligraphers all have their own individual styles and, of course, their admirers and critics, just as painters do. As calligraphy is an art with its roots in the ancient past, these scrolls are always written in the traditional way from top to bottom and usually in their full form, which is visually more pleasing. Look at the examples.

北宋　米芾　多景樓帖冊
Album of Calligraphy in
Duo Jing Lou (detail)
running script
by Mi Fu · Northern Song

元 倪瓒 渔庄秋霁图轴
Fishing Village in the Clear
Autumn Day
by Ni Zan ·Yuan

元 赵孟頫 十札卷　Ten Letters Running Script (detail)
by Zhao Mengfu·Yuan

明 沈周
仿大痴山水图轴
Landscape after Da Chi
by Shen Zhou·Ming

Look at the following couplet.

A

兩足不出門半尺
一席坐擁百城書

B

兩足不出門半尺
一席坐擁百城書

A and B are written in different styles.

Here they are again in their printed form in both full and simplified characters, with the full form on the left. The new words and translation follow. Would you be surprised if we tell you that out of the 14 characters, you have already come across 12!

兩足不出門半尺
一席坐擁百城書

两足不出门半尺
一席坐拥百城书

生词 **Shēngcí** **New words**

席	*xí*	mat, seat (cf. 主席 chairman)
拥	*yōng*	to possess (扌 hand radical)
城	*chéng*	town, city (土 earth radical)

两	足	不	出	门	半	尺
two	foot	not	out	door	half	foot (length)
一	席	坐	拥	百	城	书
one	seat	sit	have	hundred	town	book

(I) do not (have to) step out of the door half a foot,
(yet I) sit surrounded by books from a hundred towns.

And can you read the following eight characters, which run from right to left and top to bottom? You can see that two different styles are used here, too.

A 自 独 力 立 更 自 生 主

B 自 独 力 立 更 自 生 主

独立自主	to be independent and self-reliant
自力更生	to rely on one's own strength to regenerate

生词 **Shēngcí** **New words**

独	*dú*	independent, alone
立	*lì*	to stand (*a radical*)

自	*zì*	self (*a radical*)
主	*zhǔ*	to take the initiative
更	*gēng*	to change, to replace

Insight

There is no doubt that learning Chinese script will help you understand a great deal of the Chinese culture and the Chinese ways of perceiving things. Here we would like to suggest that even copying characters, which is generally regarded as a boring exercise, can help you understand some aspects of Chinese culture. Think of the words or phrases associated with learning to write Chinese characters: mechanic repetition, sticking to rules regarding stroke order, styles of calligraphy as models to follow, characters in boxes (boundaries) so that they look the same size, proportion of components, balance of parts, etc. Some people maintain that these are stereotypical characteristics of the Chinese. On the other hand the Chinese themselves will marvel at your ability to write characters, especially if you write with precision. To the Chinese, it is a sure testimony of your intelligence and talent. (The Chinese believe 字如其人, that is to say that one's handwriting is a reflection of the person in terms of his or her personality). Is it a coincidence that a character (as in a Chinese character) is the same word as a character, as in a person portrayed in an artistic piece or the qualities and features of a person?

Exercise 4

Test your recognition of 'stylized' characters. You might find this hard at first. Look at the sign below and answer the following questions.

1 Complete the characters for 'snack' and 'tea'
   中西 ＿＿ 餐、＿＿ 座

2 Write out the characters for Conference (Room)
   ＿＿ ＿＿ 厅

3 Rewrite the character after 大 in its 'normal' form.

4 What do the last four characters mean?

Seals

Seals are used for institutional as well as individual purposes such as signatures on documents (bank or post office deposits) and on paintings or scrolls. (Go back and look at the paintings and examples of calligraphy in this unit.) Just like calligraphy, seals are viewed as an art form, as they involve both design and calligraphy. The following three examples are from different dynasties.

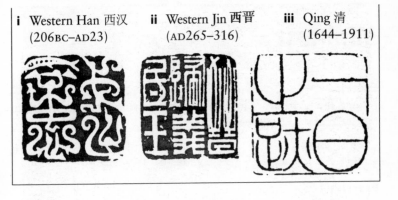

i Western Han 西汉 (206BC–AD23) **ii** Western Jin 西晋 (AD265–316) **iii** Qing 清 (1644–1911)

Points to remember

- 常 means 'often', as does 常常. While 常 is frequently used in written texts and 常常 in speech, the decision to use one or the other sometimes depends on whether the word after it is a single syllable or a disyllabic word. In the postcard, the word after 常常 is 很忙, which, although not a disyllabic word, is treated as such.

- Do you remember what 高兴 means? Yes, it means 'happy'. Do you find it surprising that the character 高 means 'high'? We don't think you should.

- When you read the Chinese weather forecast in the newspaper or on the internet, it is fairly easy to tell whether the weather will be clear/sunny or cloudy by looking at the characters 晴 and 阴 respectively because 晴 has the sun as its radical whereas 阴 contains the character for moon.

- As Chinese characters take up roughly the same space (i.e. without gaps to separate words), it is common to see slogans and public notices with coupled lines or sentences with the same number of words. You can see many such examples in this unit.

- Last but not least, being able to recognize characters and being able to write them (accurately) are two different skills. You can more or less develop one skill without paying too much attention to the other. It goes without saying that learning both skills simultaneously does ensure that the two skills complement each other and reinforces them both at the same time.

Mini-test 2

Exercise 1
Amend the word order in each of the following sentences and then put them in the correct sequence.

1 我休息中午。   **2** 我十一点睡觉晚上。

3 我四点下午去喝茶。   **4** 我起床七点一刻早上。

Exercise 2
Write the address in Chinese on an envelope to your pen pal.

> Mr Wang Mingshan*
> International University
> 9 East Lake Road
> Nanjing, China

> *míng* is 'bright', and *shān* is 'mountain'.

(Remember that the Chinese write the bigger place (i.e. the country) first and the individual person last.)

Exercise 3
Leave a notice using the following form at the reception counter of the hotel you are staying in. The notice is intended for a Chinese friend who does not read any English, telling her your whereabouts during the day in case she comes to visit you. Write in Chinese and include the following information:

- Today's date is 6 September.
- You will be at the Oriental University from 8.30 a.m. to 4.30 p.m.
- Comments: You will return to the hotel at 5 p.m.
- Your room number is 526 and your name is Helen/David King.

Where are you? 你在哪里?
Date 日期 _____
I will be at 我将在 _____
From _____ a.m./p.m. to _____ a.m./p.m.

从上午/下午 _____	至上午/下午 _____	

Comments 要求 _____

_____

Name 姓名 _____ Room No. 房号 _____

Signature 签名 _____

Peace Hotel   **西安**
Xi'an   **和平宾馆**

Exercise 4

Write a postcard in Chinese characters to your Chinese friend in Beijing saying that you really like Shanghai. The weather is sunny but often windy (有风). Tell her you are going by train to Nanjing. You are going back to your friend's in Beijing on 5 March. Tell her you miss her. (Refer back to Unit 6, Exercise 15 for some help with the vocabulary.)

Exercise 5

Look at the next few signs and see if you can give the answers for each of them.

A

百香咖啡厅
位于一楼
24小时营业

1 What is Pepper's Chinese name? Please write it out in characters.
2 Is Pepper's a restaurant?
3 Where is it situated?   4 What are its opening hours?

B

艺苑酒廊
位于二楼
早晨11:00至凌晨01:00营业

1 Where is it in the hotel?   2 What are its opening hours?

C

香怡阁
正宗粤式烹饪
位于三楼
午餐：　11:30–14:00
晚餐：　17:30–22:30

1 What sort of food does it serve? (Go back and look at Unit 8.)

2 Where is it located?　　**3** Does it serve breakfast?

D

罗马意大利餐厅
正宗意大利风味
位于三楼
晚餐：　17:30–22:30

1 What kind of restaurant is it? (see names of countries in Unit 5)

2 Where is it situated?　　**3** What meals does it serve?

Exercise 6

Look carefully at the following photos.

1 What do you think is happening at the booth, besides the advertising of Beck's beer? (The characters at the top are 游船售票处.)

2 Is the following sign advertising ice-cream, freezers or furniture?

3 Which city was the following photo taken in? Which department put up the notice? (Look up unfamiliar characters in your dictionary.)

Study the departures board below, then answer the questions.

车次	开往	时间	站台
123	南京	12点05分	12
214	西安	12点17分	4
14	上海	13点26分	6
27	北京	14点30分	9

Which platform would you go to if you wanted to go to the following cities: Beijing, Xi'an, Nanjing, Shanghai?

Exercise 8
The next two signs are strictly for fun.

Can you spot the two characters for 'delicious' in **a**? Try to write them out.

a

The proper translation for **a** would be something like this:

口香糖好吃	Chewing gum is delicious.
污渍难除	Dirty stains are difficult to get rid of.
请君莫乱吐	Please do not spit it out at random.
珍惜文物	Treasure cultural relics.

Photograph **a** is actually written in the form of a quatrain with lines 2, 3 and 4 rhyming!

b

芳草有情　盼您有义
So fragrant the lawn
So warm-hearted as you

Can you spot the character for 'grass' in **b**? The sign actually means:

The fragrant grass has feelings.
It hopes that you have righteousness (i.e. to look after it).

10

Using a Chinese–English dictionary

In this unit you will learn:

- How to use a Chinese dictionary
- About Chinese word processing
- Some more Chinese idioms

In this unit we explain how to use a Chinese–English dictionary and give you some information on Chinese word processing. We finish by explaining a little about Chinese idioms, which are so popular in both the written and spoken language.

Insight

But before we start, let's try and answer one question you might have. How many characters do you need to know to be able to read Chinese?

Well, that's not an easy question. If someone asks you how many English words one has to learn to read English texts, it's not easy to answer either.

Assuming we are talking about texts of general interest, i.e. non-technical, non-professional texts, the following is a rough guide.

Number of characters*	Coverage in percentage
50	25%
200	50%

600	80%
1000	90%
1500	95%
2500	99%

(*Most frequently used characters.)

You might be interested to know that the general criterion for literacy in China is to be able to recognize 1,500 characters.

Using a Chinese–English dictionary

Most of the dictionaries you will have access to use *pinyin* to list the characters in alphabetical order according to their pronunciation and tone. This is only of use if you know how a particular character is pronounced, otherwise you will have to look it up using the radical. (There are other systems but this is the most common and the most straightforward at this stage.) Having identified the radical (not always so easy, but refer to the **Table of radicals** for help) and counted up the number of strokes it has, you look for it in the radical index at the front of the dictionary.

We have included the radical index from a popular dictionary below (汉英词典 *A Chinese–English Dictionary*, Beijing, 1980). It may prove useful to you as a reference. The number to the left of the radical indicates its position in the character index proper.

Radicals are arranged under sub-headings according to the number of strokes they have (一画 *yī huà* one stroke, 二画 *èr huà* two strokes, 三画 *sān huà* three strokes . . . usually up to twelve and over, 十二画以上 *shí'èr huà yǐshàng*). Each radical has a number assigned to it, which may vary slightly from dictionary to dictionary – so don't automatically assume it's the same. Having found which number radical it is (the number may be to the left or to the right of the radical itself), look it up in the character index proper which immediately follows and which lists each radical in the order in which it appears in the radical index. Under each radical are listed all the characters which have that radical in common and they in turn are listed under the same sub-headings as in the radical index, 一画、二画 ... 十八画以上, i.e. the number of strokes the character has when the radical has been taken away.

Radicals with comparatively few characters assigned to them may not list each sub-heading individually but may sometimes group a few of them together, e.g. 六至八画 *liù zhì bā huà* six to eight strokes, 九至十一画 nine to eleven strokes, etc.

Thus 情 *qíng* (emotions) is listed under the heart radical 忄, under the sub-heading eight strokes 八画, and will come *after* 恨 *hèn* (hate; to hate) which comes under the sub-heading six strokes 六画, which in turn will come after 怕 *pà* (to fear) listed under five strokes 五画. Another example is 饭 *fàn* (cooked rice; food), which will come under the food radical 饣 and be listed under the sub-heading four strokes 四画 and will precede 饱 *bǎo* (have eaten one's fill, be full) which will be listed under the sub-heading five strokes 五画. We hope you have got the idea!

Let's assume you have found the character you were looking for in the index (检字表). Next to it will be either a page number, as in the Character index which we have reproduced below, or the *pinyin* and tone mark for it, either of which will enable you to look it up in the main body of the dictionary.

Remember that characters with the same pronunciation are listed with those in the first tone (indicated by ˉ) first, then those in the second tone (indicated by ´), which in turn precede those in the third (ˇ) and fourth (`) tones respectively. It sounds hard work but it's not as bad as it looks once you get the hang of it, and it can be very satisfying! It is reckoned that there are around 4,000 characters in daily use, of which approximately 2,000 are needed to get a general idea of what is going on in a newspaper.

Now try looking up three different characters in the dictionary. (We've printed the relevant pages for you: see the following pages.)

贺　　物　　氧

Step 1　Identify the radical and find it in the radical index.

Step 2　Find the radical in the character index.

Step 3 Count up the number of strokes in the character once you have taken the radical away.

Step 4 Look under the sub-heading with the corresponding number of strokes and find your character.

Step 5 Go to the page indicated and locate the character again. Bingo!

部 首 检 字
Radical Index

（一）部首目录

部首左边的号码表示部首的次序

No.	部	No.	部	No.	部	No.	部	No.	部	No.	部	No.	部
一画		35	又	70	ㅋ(彑彐)	105	ㅋ	140	丶	175	缶	209	金
1	丶	36	廴	71	弓	106	贝	141	目	176	耒	210	鱼
2	一	37	厶	72	己(巳)	107	见	142	田	177	舌	**九画**	
3	丨	38	凵	73	女	108	父	143	由	**七画**		211	音
4	丿	39	匕	74	子(孑)	109	牛(牜)	144	申	178	竹(⺮)	212	革
5	乛	**三画**		75	马	110	牛	145	皿	179	臼	213	是
6	乙	40	氵	76	幺	111	手	146	皿	180	自	214	骨
7	乙(乁乚)	41	忄	77	纟(糸)	112	毛	147	钅	181	血	215	香
二画		42	爿(丬)	78	巛	113	攵	148	矢	182	舟	216	鬼
8	冫	43	宀	**四画**		114	片	149	禾	183	羽	217	食
9	冫	44	广	79	小(⺌)	115	斤	150	白	184	艮(艮)	**十画**	
10	讠	45	门	80	灬	116	爪(爫)	151	瓜	185	言	218	高
11	二	46	辶	81	心	117	尺	152	鸟	186	辛	219	鬲
12	十	47	工	82	斗	118	月	153	皮	187	辰	220	影
13	厂	48	土(士)	83	火	119	殳	154	癶	188	麦	221	麻
14	ナ	49	艹	84	文	120	欠	155	矛	189	走	**十一画**	
15	匚	50	廾	85	方	121	风	156	疋	190	赤	222	鹿
16	卜(⺊)	51	大	86	户	122	氏	**六画**		191	豆	**十二画**	
17	刂	52	尢	87	礻	123	比	157	羊(⺶⺷)	192	束	223	黑
18	冂	53	扌	88	王	124	丰	158	关	193	酉	**十三画**	
19	冂	54	寸	89	丰	125	水	159	米	194	豕	224	鼓
20	亠	55	扌	90	天(夭)	**五画**		160	齐	195	里	225	鼠
21	亻	56	弋	91	韦	126	立	161	衣	196	足	**十四画**	
22	厂	57	巾	92	耂	127	疒	162	亦(亦)	197	采	226	鼻
23	人(入)	58	口	93	廿(卝)	128	穴	163	耳	198	豸		
24	八(丷)	59	囗	94	木	129	疋	164	臣	199	谷	227	余类
25	乂	60	山	95	不	130	皮	165	戋	200	身		
26	勹	61	屮	96	犬	131	玉	166	襾(西)	201	角		
27	刀(⺈)	62	彳	97	歹	132	示	167	束	**八画**			
28	力	63	彡	98	瓦	133	去	168	亚	202	青		
29	儿	64	夕	99	牙	134	卅	169	而	203	卓		
30	几(⺇)	65	夂	100	车	135	甘	170	页	204	雨		
31	マ	66	丸	101	戈	136	石	171	至	205	非		
32	卩	67	尸	102	止	137	龙	172	光	206	齿		
33	阝(在左)	68	饣	103	日	138	戊	173	虍	207	黾		
34	阝(在右)	69	彐	104	曰	139	业	174	虫	208	隹		

Radical index from 汉英词典 *A Chinese–English Dictionary*

Character index from 汉英词典 *A Chinese–English Dictionary*

阖 hé 〈书〉① entire; whole: ～城 the whole town/ ～家 the whole family ② shut; close: ～户 close the door

貉 hé racoon dog
另见 háo

翮 hé ① shaft of a feather; quill ② wing (of a bird): 振～高飞 flap the wings and soar high into the sky

hè

吓 hè ① threaten; intimidate ② 〈叹〉〔表示不满〕: ～怎么能干这种事呢? Tut-tut, how could you do that?
另见 xià

和 hè ① join in the singing: 一唱百～。When one starts singing, all the others join in. ② compose a poem in reply: 奉～一首 write a poem in reply (to one sent by a friend, etc., using the same rhyme sequence)
另见 hé; huó; huò

贺 hè ① congratulate ② (Hè) a surname
【贺词】 hècí speech (或 message) of congratulation; congratulations; greetings
【贺电】 hèdiàn message of congratulation; congratulatory telegram
【贺礼】 hèlǐ gift (as a token of congratulation)
【贺年】 hènián extend New Year greetings or pay a New Year call ◇ ～片 New Year card
【贺喜】 hèxǐ congratulate sb. on a happy occasion (e.g. a wedding, the birth of a child, etc.)
【贺信】 hèxìn congratulatory letter; letter of congratulation

荷 hè 〈书〉① carry on one's shoulder or back: ～锄 carry a hoe on one's shoulder/ ～枪实弹 carry a loaded rifle ② burden; responsibility: 肩负重～ shoulder heavy responsibilities ③ 〔多用于书信〕 grateful; obliged: 无任感～。I'll be very much obliged./ 请早日示复为～。An early reply will be appreciated.
另见 hé
【荷载】 hèzài load

喝 hè shout loudly: ～问 shout a question to/ 大～一声 give a loud shout
另见 hē
【喝彩】 hècǎi acclaim; cheer: 齐声～ cheer in chorus; cheer with one accord/ 博得全场～ bring the house down
【喝倒彩】 hè dàocǎi make catcalls; hoot; boo
【喝令】 hèlìng shout an order (或 command)

褐 hè ①〈书〉coarse cloth or clothing ② brown
【褐煤】 hèméi brown coal; lignite
【褐色土】 hèsètǔ drab soil
【褐铁矿】 hètiěkuàng brown iron ore; limonite
【褐藻】 hèzǎo 〈植〉 brown alga

Extract from 汉英词典 *A Chinese–English Dictionary*

务 wù ① affair; business: 公~ official business/ 任~ task; job/ 不急之~ business requiring no immediate attention; a matter of no great urgency ② be engaged in; devote one's efforts to: ~农 be engaged in agriculture; be a farmer/ 不~正业 not engage in honest work; not attend to one's proper duties ③ must; be sure to: ~使大家明了这一点 Be sure to make this point clear to everyone./ ~请光临指导 You are cordially invited to come and give guidance.
[务必] wùbì must; be sure to: 你~在本周内去看望他一次. Be sure to go and see him before the week is out.
[务实] wùshí deal with concrete matters relating to work
[务使] wùshǐ make sure; ensure
[务须] wùxū 见"务必"
[务虚] wùxū discuss principles or ideological guidelines

芴 wù <化> fluorene

坞 wù ① a depressed place: 船~ dock/ 花~ sunken flower-bed ② <书> a fortified building; castle

物 wù ① thing; matter: 废~ waste matter/ 矿~ minerals/ 公~ public property/ 以~易~ barter/ 地大~博 vast territory and rich resources ③ the outside world as distinct from oneself; other people: 待人接~ the way one gets along with people ③ content; substance: 言之无~ talk or writing devoid of substance
[物产] wùchǎn products; produce
[物故] wùgù <书> pass away; die
[物归原主] wù guī yuánzhǔ return sth. to its rightful owner

[荣华处优] yúnghuá-chǔyōu enjoy high position and live in ease and comfort; live in clover

氧 yǎng <化> oxygen (O)
[氧合作用] yǎnghé zuòyòng <生理> oxygenation
[氧化] yǎnghuà <化> oxidize; oxidate
[氧化剂] oxidizer; oxidant/ ~铁 ferric oxide/ ~物 oxide/ ~焰 oxidizing flame/ ~抑制剂 oxidation retarder (氧化抑制剂)/ ~作用 oxidation
[氧气] yǎngqì oxygen
~顶吹转炉 oxygen top-blown convertor/ ~紫铜 oxygen steelmaking/ ~面具 oxygen mask/ ~瓶 oxygen cylinder/ ~枪 <冶> oxygen lance/ ~帐 <医> oxygen tent
[氧乙炔吹管] yǎngyǐquē chuīguǎn <机> oxyacetylene blow-pipe

痒 yǎng itch; tickle: 浑身发~ itch all over/ 搔到~处 scratch where it itches — hit the nail on the head/ 怕~ ticklish
[痒痒] yǎngyang <口> itch; tickle: 蚊子咬得腿上直~. The mosquito bites on my leg itch terribly.

yàng

怏 yàng
[怏怏] yàngyàng disgruntled; sullen: ~不乐 unhappy about sth.; morose

恙 yàng <书> ailment; illness: 无~ in good health; 偶染微~ feel slightly indisposed ◇ ~螨 tsutsugamushi mite
[恙虫] yàngchóng <动> tsutsugamushi mite ~热 tsutsugamushi disease; scrub typhus

Exercise 1

For each of the following characters take out the radical and then count up the number of strokes remaining. Indicate what the radical is.

Example: 星 → 5 (日)

a 公　　b 期　　c 报　　d 场　　e 箭
f 楼　　g 电　　h 德　　i 拿　　j 室
k 路　　l 海　　m 馆　　n 旅

Exercise 2

Write a character for each of the following phonetic transcriptions so as to make a word with the character given. (You might have to check some of these in the **Vocabulary** at the back of the book.)

Example: 冰 *xiāng* → 冰(箱)

a *shàng* 午, *xià* 午　　　　b 十点 *bàn*
c 三点一 *kè*　　　　　　　　d *wǎn* 上
e *Fǎ* 国, *Zhōng* 国　　　　f 电 *yǐng*, 电 *huà*
g 啤 *jiǔ*　　　　　　　　　　h 红 *chá*
i 咖 *fēi*　　　　　　　　　　j 餐 *tīng*
k *nán* 厕所　　　　　　　　l *gōng* 共汽 *chē*, *chū* 租汽 *chēzhàn*
m 东 *běi*, *Běi* 京　　　　　n 上 *hǎi*, *Hǎinán*

Exercise 3

Translate the following passage into English. You will have to look up any unfamiliar characters in a Chinese–English dictionary:

近十年间，香港的大学生英语水准下降是人所周知的事，法律学生自不例外 . . . . . 哪知道过了九七, * 不止香港人仍在学英语，国内的人更多在学英语，原来根据统计数字，此刻中国国内在学英语的学生比在美国说英语的美国人还要多。(Taken from the Hong Kong newspaper article in Unit 9, but written in simplified characters.)

*1997, the year when Hong Kong was returned to the People's Republic of China.

Chinese word processing

No one denies that Chinese characters are more difficult to write than English and most other languages in the world. As you have read in the previous section it is more complicated to look up a character in a Chinese dictionary than to look up an English word in an English dictionary. How about word processing with a computer in this computer age?

The Chinese claim that they were the first to use letter press printing some 1,500 years ago. While in the West the use of a portable typewriter was quite common, hardly any Chinese even got near to a Chinese 'typewriter'. It was a clumsy machine. The typist had to select each lead character from a pool and punch it to print on a stencil, which was then used to print on paper. It was a very slow process!

Computers have changed the world. Typing, or writing in general for that matter, has been made much easier and faster. Some 30 years ago when computers became widely available in the West and transformed writing, many people, Chinese and Westerners alike, thought that Chinese writing was doomed in the computer age. How can a writing system as complicated as Chinese possibly be processed by a computer as fast and easily as English? Surprisingly, the answer is: it can! In fact, the number of Chinese word-processing packages available in computer software shops is increasing rapidly.

There are, broadly speaking, two main input methods. One could be termed the phonetic input method and the other the component input method.

Phonetic input method

If you are familiar with *pinyin*, the phonetic representation of the sounds in the Chinese language, this should be straightforward. Even if you are not, you have come across it many times in this book. It is the phonetic system that we have adopted throughout. Refer also to the **Pronunciation guide** for a fuller explanation.

Every character can be represented in *pinyin*, i.e. it can be given a representation of how it is supposed to sound. Logically, you can key in the *pinyin* of a character and the character should show up. This is the underlying principle of this input method. You may ask 'but what about tones and homonyms?' As you already know, there are four tones in the Modern Standard/Mandarin Chinese sound system. The same *pinyin* spelling with different tones will suggest different words. Even the same *pinyin* with the same tone would suggest different words. Such words are called homonyms. Take the sound *qing*, for example. The *Xinhua (New China) Dictionary*, the most popular pocket Chinese dictionary in China, has listed the following:

qīng 青圊清蜻鲭轻氢倾卿   *qǐng* 苘顷顸请謦

qíng 勍黥情晴氰檠擎   *qìng* 庆亲箐綮磬罄

All the characters in the same horizontal line are homonyms. When you key in *qing* in the computer, you would expect these characters to appear. You then need to select the one you want. Most *pinyin* input methods would ignore the tones and show all the characters with the same sound regardless of the tones. This is to minimize the number of keys you have to hit for a character. You will find that some of the sounds, such as *gei*, *gen* etc. have only one or two characters. Some, however, may have as many as 40 or 60 characters, such as *ji*, *xi* etc. The solution is to list characters according to their frequency in use, unlike the dictionary where characters are arranged according to radical and the number of strokes. Therefore, when you key in *qing* on the computer for the character 晴 (sunny), the following list may appear:

1 请   **2** 轻   **3** 清   **4** 青   **5** 情   **6** 晴   **7** 氢   **8** 倾   **9** 庆   **10** 擎

You then key in 6 to select 晴. If you hit the ↓ arrow key, it will give you the next ten characters, and so on.

You may have noticed that some Chinese words are formed with one character, such as 好 (good) and 大 (big), while others are formed with more than one character. For example, 朋友 (friend) and 今天 (today) both have two characters. It is therefore important to be aware that Chinese characters and English words are not equivalents. While most single characters can function as independent words on their own, most words consist of two characters, and some three characters. This is not difficult to understand. As we mentioned earlier, some 4,000 characters are used in daily life and general writing. These 4,000 characters form tens of thousands of words and expressions. Since 1900, hardly any new Chinese characters have been created, but huge numbers of new words and expressions have come into the Chinese vocabulary, and many more are still entering the language, all without the number of characters being increased.

While there are many homonyms with a single sound, there are far fewer two-character words which share exactly the same pronunciation and tone. It is precisely because of this that the Chinese word-processing system will allow you to type the *pinyin* of a whole word, such as *pengyou* and *jintian* for you to get 朋友 and 今天. There are no other words in present-day Chinese which sound exactly like *pengyou* and *jintian*. If there is more than one word with the same *pinyin*, the computer will list the options for you to choose from, in the same way as you do with an individual character. In fact when you type *pengy* for *pengyou*, 朋友 could well be there as the only candidate. Thus, a ten-stroke or even 30-stroke word can be keyed in with five or six keys. This makes the typing much faster.

This is, however, not the end of the story. Some software systems will even allow you to key in the first letter of a two-, three-, or four-character word and prompt you with the options. For example, you need key in only *py*, the first letters of *peng* and *you*, and 朋友 will appear as one of several options. As a result, you can hit three or four keys to type a 20-stroke or even 40-stroke word or phrase.

Component input method

The principle of this component input method is to deconstruct characters into a finite number of basic strokes. These basic strokes are represented by the English letters, hence correspond to the conventional keyboard. There are several software programs designed on the basis of this principle. They are all quite complex. In addition, as they are being constantly revised and updated, we feel that lengthy explanations are beyond the scope of this book. They are not easy to learn, but can be very fast to use. The advantage of this method is for those who do not speak but can read Chinese, or those who are not good at *pinyin*, the romanized system.

Chinese idioms 成语

Chinese proverbs or idioms are known as 成语 *chéngyǔ*, which are set phrases, normally made up of four characters. They are an integral part of the Chinese language. All Chinese of whatever level of education know and use 成语 and the more educated they are, the more likely they are to use them, especially in writing.

Try the next exercise to get a flavour of what 成语 are all about.

Exercise 4

Match each Chinese idiom with its correct translation. Because this is the last exercise, we've decided to make it quite a challenging one, but you have actually met almost all the characters.

1	一日千里	**a**	to say one thing and do another
2	九牛一毛	**b**	not to know how to read and write; completely illiterate
3	开门见山	**c**	one's ability falling short of one's wishes
4	力不从心	**d**	at a tremendous pace; by leaps and bounds
5	目不识丁	**e**	a drop in the ocean
6	言行不一	**f**	to put it bluntly; to come (straight) to the point; not to beat about the bush

Insight

If you have reached the end of this book, here is what we believe may be a helpful summary of common tips often given for learning Chinese script. Some of them have been mentioned in different sections of this book.

- Being able to read and being to write are different, though related, skills.
- Copying characters repeatedly may be boring but is generally very effective.
- Memorize some parts of characters, especially those meaningful ones, which are called radicals.
- A character contains three elements: the shape, the sound and the meaning. It is possible that people may only know one or two of the three elements.
- Making character cards is an effective learning method, especially for words you tend to forget and/or confuse.
- Read out loud when you look at or write a character. It helps you memorize the character.
- When you learn to read out loud (as opposed to only reading silently), it is helpful to identify the sound or phonetic component of the character.

- Find signs in Chinese and study the characters used. For example, in Chinatown, many restaurants, shops, travel agencies, beauty salons, bookshops, etc., have characters in their names. (Be careful, though, because some of them are in traditional characters, which form part of your learning of Chinese script.)
- Learn to use the computer input for Chinese characters. Write a 'pigeon' or pidgin Chinese note or e-mail to a Chinese person, i.e. an English text with some words replaced with characters that you know. After some time, your Chinese characters will grow. (Here is an example: Shall we meet at 八点二十 in 中国 town?)

祝贺你! Congratulations!

You have completed *Read and write Chinese script*. You should now have mastered the basics of written Chinese and understood how the script works. We hope you have enjoyed unravelling the mysteries of Chinese characters.

If you feel you would now like to learn to speak Chinese as well as write it, why not study *Get started in Mandarin Chinese*? If you feel you would like to advance on both fronts, then take a look at *Complete Mandarin Chinese*.

祝你走运!

Taking it further

You can find out if there are any Chinese language classes taking place in your area. Many big universities have Chinese departments or language centres which run courses in a number of foreign languages including Chinese. *Floodlight* or *Hotcourses* are such publications and they also have websites listing the courses taking place and where they are held. (*Floodlight* **http://london.floodlight.co.uk/**; *Hotcourses* **http://www.hotcourses.com/**)

You can also go online and look at the following websites, but do remember these are constantly changing and new ones are being added all the time. You can also use a search engine such as Google and type in 'Chinese characters', 'Chinese language', Chinese language courses', 'Chinese culture' and so on. This will keep you busy for a lifetime!

http://www.mandarintools.com/
A site which has many links to China-related websites.
All the instructions are in English.
English and Chinese (simplified characters).
Online English–Chinese and Chinese–English dictionary.
Illustration of stroke order.
(You can get a Chinese name by typing in your English name.)

http://www.chinese-tools.com/learn/characters
Easy to follow.

http://learningchineseonline.net/
Comprehensive. There is a section which leads you to various websites.

http://resource.chinese.cn/en/
网络孔子学院 Comprehensive. There is a section for learning characters.

Key to the exercises

Unit 1

Exercise 1

a No smoking   **b** Coffee shop
c No U turn   **d** No photography
e Petrol/gas station   **f** No swimming
g Wheelchair access

Exercise 2

车: 1E, 2B, 3D, 4A   马: 1A, 2C, 3E, 4B
鱼: 1D, 2A, 3F, 4C   雨: 1C, 2E, 3B, 4D
山: 1B, 2F, 3C, 4E   子: 1F, 2D, 3A, 4F

Exercise 3

1 月 moon   2 木 wood/tree   3 山 mountain
4 雨 rain   5 日 sun   6 鱼 fish
7 马 horse   8 车 vehicle   9 子 child
10 人 person

Test yourself

1 **b** Hong Kong   **c** Taiwan
2 **a** the sun
3 **b** 人
4 **c** 车
5 **a** 馬

Unit 2

Exercise 2

信 letter, 鲜 fresh, 安 peace, stability

Exercise 3

从 to follow, 众 crowd, 林 wood (smaller than forest, less wild),
森 forest, 炎 burning hot, 焱 flame

Exercise 4

1 骡、驴、驹 2 花、草、芽 3 钢、锈、铃 4 逃、过、迈

Exercise 5

1 打 2 灶 3 讥 4 雪

Exercise 6

1 泪 tears 2 林 wood, forest 3 笔 pen, brush

4 囚 prisoner 5 灾 disaster

Exercise 7

墙 wall, 扔 to throw, 怕 fear, 汗 sweat, 吻 kiss, 椅 chair,
暖 warm, 她 she

Test yourself

1 囚 2 田 3 男
4 Left 5 True 6 True

7 False (many don't)

Unit 3

Exercise 1

1 人 丿人 2 田 丨冂冂田田
3 大 一ナ大 4 木 一十才木
5 车 丿ノ左车车 6 山 丨山山
7 忄丨忄忄 *or* 心 丿心心心 8 言 丶亠亠言言言言

Exercise 2

刂	小	材	少	尘	你
丷	心	言	家	米	兴
冫	打	河	冰	牲	跑
丿	力	长	火	户	石
一	大	香	草	鱼	马

Exercise 3

1 月 丿 几 月 月

2 牛 丿 ㇑ 二 牛

3 户 丶 ㇈ ㇕ 户

4 穴 丶 丷 宀 宀 穴

5 当 丨 ⺌ ⺌ 当 当 当

6 米 丶 丷 ⺌ 半 米 米

Exercise 4

A b C D e F

Exercise 5

A Top too big (鱼)

B 日 on the left should be smaller than 月 on the right (明)

C Gap between the two components is too big (休)

D Top too small (男)

E Roof much too big (安)

F The door should be open, i.e. there is a space between the dot and 冂 (门)

G The third stroke of the water radical should be rising, i.e. 氵 and not 丶 (泪)

H The vertical should not extend into the box (草)

Exercise 6

b

Exercise 7

1 目: eye

2 犭: animal

3 饣: food

4 刂: knife

5 山: mountain

Exercise 8

Radicals:

1 木 wood/tree

2 言 讠 speech

3 山 mountain

4 氵 water

5 日 sun

6 灬 fire

7 贝 money

8 火 fire

9 ⺮ bamboo

10 刂 knife

Characters: example: 话 speech, language

1 枫 maple

2 讽 to mock

3 峰 peak

4 海 sea

5 晚 evening, late

6 煮 to boil

130

7 资 capital   **8** 烧 to burn

9 笔 brush pen   **10** 刻 to carve

Exercise 9

Radical table stroke order   刂:丨刂;   刀:ノ刀;   石:一ア丆石石;
饣:ノ𠂉饣;   食:ノ人𠆢今今今食食食食;   口:丨冂口;   目:丨冂冂月月目;
贝:丨冂贝贝;   氵:丶冫氵;   水:丿水水水;   见:丨冂贝见;   牛:ノ𠂇牛牛;
页:一ナ丆丏页页;   彳:ノ彳彳;   米:丶丷丬半米米

Exercise 10

1 马 (horse) on the left-hand side   **2** 艹 (grass/plant) on the top
3 犭 (animal) on the left   **4** 讠 (speech) on the left
5 灬 (fire) at the bottom   **6** 竹 (bamboo) on the top
7 氵 (water) on the left   **8** 刂 (knife) on the right
9 亻 (person) on the left   **10** 口 (mouth) can be anywhere

Exercise 11

1 泪 tear   **2** 林 wood, forest   **3** 笔 (brush) pen
4 囚 prisoner   **5** 灾 disaster   **6** 尘 dust
7 晃 dazzling

Exercise 12

1 氵 water 泪汗河   **2** 讠 speech 诗 说 词 订
3 木 wood/tree 杂 林 根 材   **4** 刂 knife 别 刚 刷
5 扌 hand 打 推 扣   **6** 日 sun/day 昨 时 晚
7 饣 food 饭 饺 饿   **8** 贝 shell 货 贡 贵
9 口 mouth 吸 吃 叮 喝

Exercise 13

方(4) 丶一亍方;   山(3) 丨山山;   九(2) 乀九 or 丿九;
足(7) 丨冂口𠯜𠯜足足;   去(5) 一十土去去;   气(4) 丿𠂉气气;
尺(4) ㇇彐尸尺;   风(4) 丿几风风

Test yourself

1 The horizontal stroke
2 The bottom horizontal line
3 Three
4 Three

5 The vertical stroke in the middle

6 米. The Chinese say 米字旗: the flag (旗) with the 米 character (字).

7 Yes

Unit 4

Exercise 1

1 小心 to be careful

2 放心 to feel at ease

3 瞎话 lie (noun)

4 笑话 joke (noun)

Exercise 2

1 火车 train

2 木工 carpentry, carpenter

3 月票 monthly pass

4 电视 television

5 电车 trolley bus

6 电影 film

7 电脑 computer

Exercise 3

1 好吃 delicious

2 难听 unpleasant to listen to

3 好看 good-looking

4 难看 ugly

Exercise 4

1 大学 university   **2** 小费 tip, gratuity   **3** 好心 kind-hearted

Exercise 5

公平 **a** to be fair; justice

明天 **c** tomorrow

Exercise 6

1 吃饭 to eat

2 教书 to teach

3 录音 to record

4 走路 to walk

5 说话 to speak

Exercise 7

a 4	**b** 8	**c** 5	**d** 7
e 9	**f** 6	**g** 10	**h** 18
i 35	**j** 94	**k** 76	**l** 59

Exercise 8

a 八	**b** 十	**c** 七	**d** 五
e 六	**f** 九	**g** 四	**h** 二十一
i 三十二	**j** 八十七	**k** 六十五	**l** 九十四

132

Exercise 9

a 1919	**b** 1991	**c** 1945
d 1066	**e** 1789	**f** 1914
g 1492	**h** 1848	**i** 2015

Exercise 10

a 一三二一	**b** 一九三二	**c** 一八七六
d 一九六五	**e** 一九四九	**f** 一四八六
g 一九三七	**h** 一八四二	**i** 二〇三七

Exercise 11

a 1 February	**b** 7 March	**c** 9 May
d 10 April	**e** 20 June	**f** 30 August
g 26 November	**h** 15 October	**i** 31 December

Exercise 12

a = 6; **b** = 8; **c** = 4; **d** = 2; **e** = 1; **f** = 9; **g** = 5; **h** = 7; **i** = 3

Exercise 13

| **a** 一月一日 | **b** 四月二十三日 | **c** 七月四日 |
| **d** 十二月二十五日 | **e** 六月二十一日 | |

Exercise 14

International Women's Day is on 8 March.

Exercise 15

a = 3; **b** = 6; **c** = 1; **d** = 7; **e** = 2; **f** = 5; **g** = 4

Exercise 16

a 星期五 **b** 星期日 **c** 星期六

Mini-test 1

Exercise 1

1 情 *qíng* = **d** feeling (heart radical)
2 清 *qīng* = **g** clear (water radical)
3 鲭 *qīng* = **f** mackerel (fish radical)
4 请 *qǐng* = **a** to ask, request (speech radical)
5 蜻 *qīng* = **b** dragonfly (insect radical)
6 晴 *qíng* = **c** bright/sunny day (sun/day radical)
7 氰 *qíng* = **e** cyanogen (air radical)

Exercise 2

1 = **c** (cf. 大 big; great); **2** = **e**; **3** = **d** (cf. 日 day; daily); **4** = **b**;
5 = **a** (cf. 土 (earth) radical in 场)

Exercise 3

1 生日 **b** birthday   **2** 早安   **c** good morning
3 日历 **b** calendar

Exercise 4

早	上	上	午	中	午	下	午	晚	上

Exercise 5

不公平 means 'not fair, unfair'. The left-hand side is menswear.

Exercise 6

a 中学 secondary school,   中国 China,   中心 centre,   中午 noon
b 火腿 ham, 火山 volcano, 火车 train, 火箭 rocket, 火花 spark

Exercise 7

a mouth 口	**b** rain 雨	**c** fire (2) 火 灬
d page 页	**e** wind 风	**f** knife (2) 刀 刂
g rice 米	**h** child 子	**i** metal (2) 金 钅
j eye 目	**k** horse 马	**l** speech (2) 言 讠
m big 大	**n** field 田	**o** heart (2) 心 忄
p woman 女	**q** mountain 山	**r** step with left foot 彳
s door 门	**t** to walk 辶	

Unit 5

Exercise 1

			Radical	Meaning
a 匕、又	**b**	i 饭	饣	food
		ii 楼	木	wood/tree
		iii 楼	米 女	rice, woman
		iv 员	贝	shell
		v 迎	辶	

c (木) 、、丷丷屵屵弟弟(梯)   **d** 女; 女; 一/口; 女

Exercise 2

电梯 lift, elevator,   店员 shop assistant,   服务楼 service block,
电台 radio station

Exercise 3
A 广东餐厅　　**B** 四川餐厅　　**ii** Not to smoke

Exercise 4
1 山田　**2** 美国 USA　**3** 英国 UK　**4** 法国 France　**5** No　**6** 刘

Exercise 5
A 国安　　**B** 大明　　**C** 英林　　**D** 京生

Exercise 6
a 09.00–17.00　　　　**b** 7 a.m.–11 p.m.
c 08.30–19.00　　　　**d** 8.00 a.m.–12.00 noon, 2.00–6.00 p.m.

Exercise 7
a 八　**b** 刂　**c** 丶　**d** 耂　**e** 羊

Exercise 8
a 三点二十　　　　　　**b** 十点四十五, 十点三刻, 差一刻十一点
c 九点半　　　　　　　**d** 四点五十, 差十分五点
e 一点一刻　　　　　　**f** 七点三十五

Exercise 9
The radicals are in brackets: 程(禾), 表(一), 第(⺮), 早(日), 上(一), 中(丨), 午(丿), 下(一), 晚(日), 开(一), 会(人), 参(厶), 观(见), 海(氵), 公(八), 园(囗)

Exercise 10
1 Shanghai Restaurant 上海餐厅
2 12.00–13.00 十二点--一点
3 See the film 'Sunrise' 电影《日出》
4 1.30 p.m. 一点半
5 8.30–11.30 a.m. and 1.30–4.00 p.m. 上午八点半--十一点半, 下午一点半--四点
6 Visiting Beihai (North Sea) Park 参观北海公园
7 A university 大学 (Qinghua University 清华大学)

Exercise 11
啤酒 (口氵) (beer) 葡萄酒 (⺾ ⺾ 氵) (wine) (*lit.* grape alcohol) 可口可乐 (口 口 口 木) (Coca-Cola) 咖啡 (口 口) (coffee) 茶 (⺾) (tea) 矿泉水 (石 水 水) (mineral water)

Exercise 12
a Bar, beverage, food　　　　**b** 咖啡、饮料、啤酒

Exercise 13

1 French restaurant
2 Men's toilets
3 Women's toilets
4 Lift/elevator
5 Stairs
6 Japanese restaurant
7 Telephone
8 Reception
9 Entrance and exit
10 Bar

Test yourself

1 **a** It comes first
2 **b** The ground floor

Unit 6

Revision exercise

出 2	下 3	华 10	梯 6	北 2	河 9
湖 9	园 5	二 3	上 3	法 9	东 3
南 10	楼 6	香 8	晚 1	弟 4	分 7
半 4	三 3	共 2	海 9	李 6	十 10
星 1	公 7	汽 9	国 5	程 8	中 2

1 日 sun
2 丨 vertical
3 一 horizontal/one
4 丶 dot
5 囗 enclosure
6 木 wood/tree
7 八 eight
8 禾 grain
9 氵 water
10 十 ten

Exercise 1

1 East
2 First go northeast and then north
3 Immediate north
4 Go straight east
5 Southeast corner of the park

Exercise 2

1 Beijing
2 Shanghai
3 Nanjing
4 Xi'an
5 Hong Kong
6 Taiwan
7 Hainan
8 Donghai (East China Sea)
9 Nanhai (South China Sea)
10 Tibet

Exercise 3

1 中东 Middle East **2** 地中海 the Mediterranean

3 南美 South America **4** 北海 North Sea

Exercise 4

1 Zhongshan Bei Lu 中山北路 **c** **2** Ren He Lu 仁和路 **a**

3 Ping Hai Lu 平海路 **b**

Exercise 5

a Southeast **b** Northwest

c 南京 (*lit.* south capital) Nanjing

Exercise 6

a = iii **b** = iv **c** = ii **d** = i

Exercise 7

3 and 5 are in full form.

a = 3 **b** = 5 **c** = 6 **d** = 4 **e** = 2 **f** = 1 **g** = 7

Exercise 8

a No smoking **b** No admission **c** No parking

Exercise 9

a 请勿照相 (No photography) 昭 > 照; fire ⺣ radical for 'to shine' or 'to flash'.

b 小心触电 (Danger: Electric shock) 解 > 触; 触 means 'to touch'. It consists of a 角 (antenna/horn) and a 虫 (insect), i.e. like the antenna of an insect.

c 请勿吸烟 (No smoking) 咽 > 烟; fire 火 radical for 'smoke'.

d 请勿随地吐痰 (No spitting) 灶 > 吐; mouth 口 radical for 'spitting'.

Exercise 10

a 娄 > 楼 radical 木 represents 'wood/tree'

b 艮 > 银 radical 钅 represents 'metal'

c 酉 > 酒 radical 氵 represents 'water'

d 反 > 饭 radical 饣 represents 'food'

Exercise 11

a 火车站 **b** 葡萄酒 **c** 矿泉水 **d** 服务员

Exercise 12

禁止停车 No parking; 法国银行 Bank of France; 北京大学 Beijing University; 开往上海 Shanghai-bound train

Exercise 13

1 六   2 京   3 会   4 点   5 半   6 上
7 刻   8 影   9 星   10 观   11 园

Exercise 14

The correct order is: 3, 4, 1, 5, 2

Exercise 15

I stayed at the Nanjing Hotel for four days. On the first day, the attendant said: 'Welcome to the Nanjing Hotel.' I stayed on the second floor (UK). The next day I visited Xuanwu Lake Park in the morning, and visited Dr Sun Yatsen's Mausoleum in the afternoon. I watched a film in the evening. On the third and fourth days I attended meetings at Nanjing University. At noon on the third day we had lunch in a Cantonese restaurant. At noon on the fourth day we had lunch in a Shanghainese restaurant. The food in both restaurants was delicious. I had breakfast at 7 a.m. on the morning of the fifth day. At 7.45 I took a taxi to the railway station and went back to Beijing on the 8.10 train.

Test yourself

1 出 '(to go) out'   2 export
3 公 'public'   4 b use
5 a 东北   6 b 东西南北
7 a The east capital

Unit 7

Exercise 1

a = 6 b = 4 c = 2 d = 8 e = 7 f = 9 g = 5 h = 10 i = 3
j = 1; iv is in full-form characters (區 for 区 and 書 for 书).

Exercise 2

1 A restaurant (the Shandong Restaurant)
2 E   3 G   4 A
5 Kentucky Fried Chicken   6 F

Exercise 3

a Konica;   b Kentucky Fried Chicken;

c Beck's Beer; **d** Chunlan Freezers;

e Cornetto; **d** is the odd one out (it's a Chinese brand).

Exercise 4

a; **b** is a better road

Exercise 5

a International (breakfast) **b** American (breakfast)

c Continental (breakfast) **d** Chinese (breakfast)

e Breakfast **f** 式

g Style, type

h Fill in your name, number of people, signature, room number and the date.

Exercise 6

a You ticked 苹果汁、煎双面蛋、火腿、多士、咖啡

b Fresh fruit yoghurt **c** 新鲜水果伴酸奶

d 服务费 **e** ￥11.7

Exercise 7

	很好	好	一般	差
广东餐厅		✓		
四川餐厅	✓			
送餐服务			✓	

Exercise 8

Flight Confirmation Request		航班确认申请
Surname	First name	Room No.
姓 _____	名 _____	房号 _____
Airline	Departure Date	Passport No.
航空公司 _____	离开日期 _____	护照号码 _____
Flight No.	Take-Off time	
航班号 _____	起飞时间 _____	
Destination		
目的地 _____		
Remarks		
备注 _____		
Date	Signature	Received by
日期 _____	客人签名 _____	接收人 _____

Exercise 9

1 = e **2** = c **3** = f **4** = a **5** = d **6** = b. GITIC Plaza Hotel is in Guangzhou (Canton).

Exercise 10

i No **ii** 3, 5, 6 **iii** Full form (園 for 园 and 飯 for 饭)
iv At the beginning **v** 3 and 6 **vi** 1 and 4
vii 3 and 6 (Hotel Equatorial and Yangtze New World Hotel)

Exercise 11

a 航空 means 'airmail' **b** 邮票 means 'postage stamp(s)'
c 及 means 'and' **d** 寄 means 'to post' or 'to mail'
e 收件人、寄件人

Test yourself

1 纟 'silk' **2** 店 'shop'
3 品 *pǐn* 'product, to taste' **4** 餐 *cān* 'food/meal'
5 差 *chà* 'to lack; missing' **6** 国 *guó*
7 土 'earth/land'

Unit 8

Exercise 1

a Red Mansion Cinema
b Big Shanghai
c Letter from the South
d Letter from the South and Red River Valley

Exercise 2

a Upstairs **b** Even numbers **c** 7.45 **d** 20 June

Exercise 3

a Westbound, 7 stops **b** Westbound, 2 stops
c Westbound, 5 stops **d** Eastbound, 2 stops

Exercise 4

1 Beijing University **2** 20 yuan
3 Electric appliances **4** English

5 7 days

6 The British Education Exhibition and the English Book Fair

7 The Japanese Electric Appliances Fair

Exercise 5

a 姓名 Name   **b** 中文 Chinese

c 英文 English   **d** 性别 Sex

e 出生年月 Date of birth 年 year 月 month 日 day

f 现住址 Current address

g 电话 Telephone   **h** 工作单位 Place of work

Exercise 6

a 8 West Lake Road 西湖路八号

b The Oriental Hotel 东方饭店

c The Children's Amusement Park 儿童乐园

d The People's Park 人民公园

Exercise 7

饭 丿 亅 钅 饣 饣 饣 饭 饭 (饣)

楼 一 十 才 才 木 杉 档 档 杵 楼 楼 楼 (木)

河 丶 冫 氵 沪 沪 沪 河 河 (氵)

院 乛 阝 阝 阝 阮 阮 院 院 院 (阝)

场 一 十 土 圫 圽 场 场 (土)

Exercise 8

a 目的地   **b** 7 June, 9:40 a.m.   **c** Rear door

Exercise 9

a 香港 means Hong Kong (*lit.* fragrant harbour) (see Unit 5)

b Yes   **c** Yes, beef

d 或   **e** Fresh fruit

f Black tea, Japanese green tea, Chinese tea and coffee

Exercise 10

a Twice

b Two hours before landing

c 服务员

d 小吃 are snacks (*lit.* small eat/food)

e Dinner

f 三文治 (*sānwénzhì*) means 'sandwich'

g Fruit juice (cf. water radical)

Unit 9

Exercise 1

一心一意 whole-hearted(ness), with undivided attention; 三心二意 to be in two minds; 一心二用 not giving undivided attention to something; 三言两语 (of speech) brief; 七上八下 to be in a state of anxiety and nervousness; 百年大计 a project of vital and far-reaching importance; 千山万水 (covering) a vast area of land; 千家万户 every family and household; 千言万语 (there is) a great deal to express

Exercise 2

1 During the day

2 a From the south   **b** From the northwest

3 In the evening

4 In the evening

5 28 April

Exercise 3

1 和平饭店 the Peace Hotel   **2** Delicious

3 Beijing   **4** The Great Hall of the People

5 Beijing   **6** Nanjing

7 To wish her a Happy Valentine's Day

8 Xi'an

9 15 January 1998

Exercise 4

1 中西快餐、茶座   **2** 会议厅

3 众   **4** Telephone number for reservations

Mini-test 2

Exercise 1

1 我中午休息   **2** 我晚上十一点睡觉

3 我下午四点去喝茶   **4** 我早上七点一刻起床

The correct sequence is 4, 1, 3, 2.

Exercise 2

中国南京　　东湖路九号　　国际大学　　王明山　　收

Exercise 3

<table>
<tr><td colspan="3" align="center">**Where are you?**　　你在哪里？</td></tr>
<tr><td>Date 日期</td><td colspan="2">九月六日</td></tr>
<tr><td>I will be at 我将在</td><td colspan="2">东方大学</td></tr>
<tr><td>From</td><td>a.m./p.m. to</td><td>a.m./p.m.</td></tr>
<tr><td>从 上午/下午</td><td>八点半</td><td>至上午/下午　四点半</td></tr>
<tr><td>Comments 要求</td><td colspan="2"></td></tr>
<tr><td colspan="3" align="center">我下午五点回饭店</td></tr>
<tr><td>Name 姓名</td><td>王海伦/王大卫</td><td>Room No. 房号　526</td></tr>
<tr><td>Signature 签名</td><td colspan="2"></td></tr>
<tr><td colspan="3" align="center">Peace Hotel　　西安
Xi'an　　和平宾馆</td></tr>
</table>

Exercise 4

我很喜欢上海。 天气很好， 可是常常有风。 我要坐火车去南京。
三月五号回北京。 我想你。

Exercise 5

A 1 百香　2 No, it's a café　3 Ground floor (UK), 1st floor (US)　4 It's open 24 hours

B 1 1st floor (UK), 2nd floor (US)　2 11.00 a.m.–1.00 a.m.

C 1 Cantonese food　2 2nd floor (UK), 3rd floor (US)　3 No

D 1 Italian　2 2nd floor (UK), 3rd floor (US)　3 Dinner

Exercise 6

1 Boat tickets are being sold

2 Freezers

3 Hangzhou, the local tax office

Exercise 7

Beijing (9), Xi'an (4), Nanjing (12), Shanghai (6)

Exercise 8

a 好吃　　b 草

Unit 10

Exercise 1

a 2 (八)　　**b** 8 (月)　　**c** 4 (扌)　　**d** 3 (土)　　**e** 9 (灬)
f 9 (木)　　**g** 4 (乚/彐)　**h** 12 (亻)　**i** 6 (手)　　**j** 6 (宀)
k 6 (足)　　**l** 7 (讠)　　**m** 8 (彳)　　**n** 6 (方)

Exercise 2

a (上)午, (下)午　　**b** 十点(半)　　　　**c** 三点一(刻)
d (晚)上　　　　　　**e** (法)国, (中)国　　**f** 电(影), 电(话)
g 啤(酒)　　　　　　**h** 红(茶)　　　　　　**i** 咖(啡)
j 餐(厅)　　　　　　**k** (男)厕所
l (公)共汽(车), (出)租汽(车站)
m 东(北), (北)京　　**n** 上(海), (海南)

Exercise 3

In the last ten years, the fact that the standard of English of Hong Kong's university students has fallen is something that is known to everyone; students of law are no exception . . . Who would have thought that, after 1997, not only do Hong Kong people still study English but also even more people within China are doing so? In fact, according to statistics, the number of students learning English in China at this present moment is even greater than the number of Americans speaking English in America.

Exercise 4

1 = d,　**2** = e,　**3** = f,　**4** = c,　**5** = b,　**6** = a

Table of radicals

You will find slight variations in the radical indexes of different dictionaries. See below a list of most of the one- or two-stroke radicals, which do not necessarily carry any meaning. If they do, this does not normally help your understanding of the meaning of the character of which they are the radical. They are, however, indispensable for looking up characters in a dictionary.

> 丶 一 丨 丿 乛 乙 乛 乚 儿 厂 匚 卜 冂 厂 乂 勹 凵 厶

The number in the right-hand column below indicates the unit in which the radical first appears.

			Unit
二画			
冫(冰)	*bīng*	ice	4
亠		above	5
讠(言)	*yán*	speech	2
二	*èr*	two	4
十	*shí*	ten	4
刂(刀)	*dāo*	knife	3
亻(人)	*rén*	person	2
人(亻)	*rén*	person	1
八(丷)	*bā*	eight	4
刀(刂)	*dāo*	knife	3
力	*lì*	strength	2

儿	ér	child; son	7
阝(LHS)		mound	5
阝(RHS)		town, region	5
又	yòu	again	5
三画			
氵(水)	shuǐ	water	3
忄(心)	xīn	heart	2
广	guǎng	covering, roof	4
宀		roof	2
门	mén	door	4
辶		to walk (quickly)	2
工	gōng	work	2
土	tǔ	earth	2
艹	cǎo	grass	2
大	dà	big	2
寸	cùn	inch	5
扌(手)	shǒu	hand	2
巾	jīn	towel, napkin	8
口	kǒu	mouth	3
囗		enclosure	2
山	shān	mountain	1
彳		step with left foot	3
饣(食)	shí	food	3
犭	quǎn	(wild) animal, dog	3

女	nǚ	woman	2
子	zǐ	child	1
马	mǎ	horse	1
纟	sī	silk	4
小	xiǎo	small	2
四画			
灬 (火)	huǒ	fire	2
心 (忄)	xīn	heart	2
火 (灬)	huǒ	fire	2
方	fāng	square	5
户	hù	household	2
礻		omen; to express	5
王	wáng	king	4
天	tiān	sky, heaven, day	4
木	mù	wood, tree	1
车	chē	vehicle	1
戈	gē	spear	5
日	rì	sun, day	1
贝	bèi	shell	3
见	jiàn	see	3
父	fù	father	5
气	qì	air	4
牛 (牜)	niú	cattle	3
手 (扌)	shǒu	hand	2

毛	*máo*	fur, hair	2
攵		to tap; rap	5
斤	*jīn*	half a kilogram	8
月*	*yuè*	moon; flesh	4
风	*fēng*	wind	4
水 (氵)	*shuǐ*	water	3

月* Characters with the 'moon' and 'flesh' radical are no longer differentiated and appear under the same radical 月. 'Flesh' as a character in its own right is written 肉 and is pronounced *ròu*.

五画			
立	*lì*	to stand	5
疒		illness	5
穴	*xué*	cave	4
衤(衣)	*yī*	clothing	4
玉	*yù*	jade	5
石	*shí*	stone; mineral	2
目	*mù*	eye	3
田	*tián*	field	2
钅(金)	*jīn*	metal (gold)	2
禾	*hé*	grain, plant	4
鸟	*niǎo*	bird (long-tailed)	5
六画			
羊	*yáng*	sheep	2
米	*mǐ*	(uncooked) rice	3
衣(衤)	*yǐ*	clothing	4

页	yè	page	3
虫	chóng	insect	4
舌	shé	tongue	2
竹 (⺮)	zhú	bamboo	2
舟	zhōu	boat	5

七画

言 (讠)	yán	speech	2
走	zǒu	to go, walk	5
酉	yǒu	spirit made from ripe millet; Tenth of Twelve Earthly Branches	5
豕	shǐ	pig	2
足	zú	foot	5

八画

雨	yǔ	rain	1
金 (钅)	jīn	gold (metal)	2
鱼	yú	fish	1

九画

食 (饣)	shí	food	3

Pronunciation guide

Chinese sounds

Vowels

Here is the list of the Chinese vowels with a rough English equivalent sound, and then one or two examples in Chinese. There are single vowels, compound vowels or vowels plus a nasal sound which will be listed separately.

	rough English sound	Chinese examples
a	father	baba, mama
ai	bite	tai, zai
ao	cow	hao, zhao
e	fur	che, he, ge
ei	play	bei, gei, shei, fei
i	tea	didi, feiji, ni
i	*	zi, ci, shi

*after z, c, s, zh, ch, sh and r only. The i is there more or less for cosmetic reasons – no syllable can exist without a vowel. Say the consonant and 'sit on it' and you have the sound.

ia	yam	jia, xia
iao	meow	biao, piao, yao
ie	yes	bie, xie, ye
iu	yo-yo	liu, jiu, you

y replaces **i** at the beginning of a word if there is no initial consonant.

o	m**o**re	m**o**yim**o**, map**o**
ou	g**o**	d**ou**, z**ou**
u	m**oo**	b**u**, zh**u**
ua	s**ua**ve	g**ua**, h**ua**
uo	w**ar**	sh**uo**, c**uo**, **wo**
uai	sw**i**pe	k**uai**, **wai**
ui	**weigh**	d**ui**, g**ui**, z**ui**

w replaces **u** at the beginning of a word if there is no initial consonant.

ü	pne**u**monia	j**u**, q**u**, l**ü**, n**ü**
üe	pne**u**matic + **air** (said quickly)	**yue**, x**ue**, j**ue**

Note that ü and üe can occur only with the consonants n, l, j, q and x. As j, q and x cannot occur as j+u, q+u or x+u, the umlaut (¨) over the 'u' in **ju**, **qu** and **xu** has been omitted. n and l, however, can occur as both **nu** and **nü**, **lu** and **lü** so the umlaut (¨) has been kept.

yu replaces ü, and yue replaces üe if there is no initial consonant.

Here are the **vowels with a nasal sound** formed with vowels followed by **n** or **ng**. Speak through your nose when you pronounce them.

	rough English sound	Chinese examples
an	m**an**	f**an**, m**an**
ang	b**ang**	zh**ang**, sh**ang**
en	**un**der	r**en**, h**en**
eng	h**ung**	d**eng**, n**eng**
in	b**in**	n**in**, j**in**, x**in**
ian	**yen**	t**ian**, n**ian**, q**ian**
iang	**Yang**tze (River)	l**iang**, x**iang**

ing	finger	ming, qing, xing
iong	**Jung** (the psychoanalyst)	yong, qiong, xiong
ong	Jung	tong, cong, hong
uan	wangle	wan, suan, huan
un	won	wen, lun, chun
uang	wrong	wang, huang, zhuang
üan	pneumatic + end (said quickly)	yuan, quan, xuan
ün	'une' in French	yun, jun, qun

Note that **ian** is pronounced as if it were i**e**n.

The same rules about **y** replacing **i** and **w** replacing **u** at the beginning of a word if there is no initial consonant also apply to vowels with a nasal sound.

Yuan replaces **üan** and **yun** replaces **ün** if there is no initial consonant.

Consonants

Here is a list of the Chinese consonants: some of them are quite similar to English sounds, others less so. Those that are very different from the nearest English sound are explained.

	rough English sound	Chinese examples
b	**b**ore	**b**ai, **b**ei
p	**p**oor	**p**ao, **p**ang
m	**m**e	**m**a, **m**ei, **m**ing
f	**f**an	**f**an, **f**eng
d	**d**oor	**d**a, **d**ou, **d**uo
t	**t**ore	**t**a, **t**ai, **t**ian
n	**n**eed	**n**a, **n**ü, **n**ian

l	lie	lai, lei, liang
z	adds	zi, zai, zuo
c	its	ci, cai, cuo
s	say	si, sui, suan

The next four consonants are all made with the tongue loosely rolled in the middle of the mouth.

zh	jelly	zhao, zhong, zhu
ch	chilly	che, chi, chang
sh	shy	shi, shei, sheng
r	razor	re, ri, rong

The next three consonants are all made with the tongue flat and the corners of the mouth drawn back as far as possible.

j	genius	jia, jiao, jian
q	cheese (as said in front of the camera!)	qi, qian, qu
x	sheet (rather like a whistling kettle)	xiao, xin, xue

Arch the back of the tongue towards the roof of the mouth for the last three consonants.

g	guard	ge, gei, gui
k	card	kai, kan, kuai
h	loch	he, hai, hao

Tones

Chinese is a tonal language. Every syllable in Chinese has its own tone. **Pǔtōnghuà** has four distinct tones plus a neutral tone. This means that syllables which are pronounced the same but have different tones will mean different things. For example, **tang** pronounced in the first tone means *soup*, but pronounced in the second tone means *sugar*! But don't worry – all the four tones fall within your natural voice range. You don't have to have a particular type of voice to speak Chinese.

The four tones are represented by the following marks, which are put over the vowel, such as **nǐ** *you*, or over the main vowel of a syllable where there are two or three vowels, e.g. **hǎo** *good*, but **guó** *country*:

— 1st tone, high and level

/ 2nd tone, rising

V 3rd tone, falling–rising

\ 4th tone, falling

The diagrams below will help to make this clearer.

Think of **1** as being at the bottom of your voice range and **5** at the top.

1st tone: Pitch it where **you** feel comfortable. Say 'oo' as in 'zoo' and keep going for as long as you can. You should be able to keep it up for maybe half a minute. When you have got used to that, change to another vowel sound and practise that in the same way and so on.

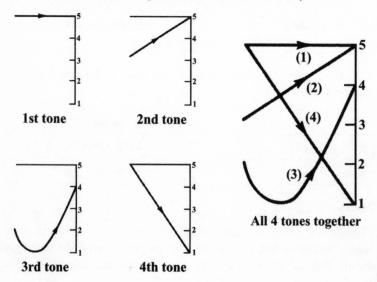

1st tone   2nd tone

3rd tone   4th tone

All 4 tones together

2nd tone: Raise your eyebrows every time you attempt a second tone until you get used to it. This is infallible!

3rd tone: Drop your chin onto your neck and raise it again. Then practise the sound doing the movement at the same time.

4th tone: Stamp your foot gently and then accompany this action with the relevant sound.

Neutral tones: Some syllables in Chinese are toneless or occur in the neutral tone. This means they have no tonemark over the vowel. They are rather like unstressed syllables in English, such as *of a* in 'two of a kind'.

Tone changes
Occasionally syllables may change their tones.

a Two 3rd tones, one after another, are very difficult to say. Where this happens, the first one is said as a 2nd tone:
Nǐ hǎo! (*How do you do?*) is said as **Ní hǎo.**

b If three 3rd tones occur together, the first two are normally said as 2nd tones:
Wǒ yě hǎo (*I'm OK too*) is said as **Wó yé hǎo.**

Useful public signs and notices

Time

营业时间	Business hours
办公时间	Office hours

Public signs

静	Quiet
推	Push
拉	Pull
开门	Open door (as in lifts/elevators)
关门	Close door (as in lifts/elevators)
欢迎	Welcome
入口	Entrance
出口	Exit
男厕所	Men's toilets/Gentlemen
女厕所	Women's toilets/Ladies
洗手间	Toilet (*lit.* washing hands room)
存车处	Bicycle compound
谢绝参观	Not open to visitors
闲人免进	Admittance to staff only
游客止步	Not open to tourists/Visitors keep out
凭票入内	Admission by ticket only
免费入场	Admission free
小心触电	Danger: Electric shock
禁止停车	No parking
禁止通行	No entry
请勿吸烟	No smoking
请勿照相	No photography
自行车修理部	Bicycle repairs
黄线范围内禁止停放车辆	No parking within the yellow lines

Shopping

商城	Shopping centre, shopping mall
百货商店	Department store
市场	Market
超级市场	Supermarket
收款台/收银	Cashier
大减价	Big reductions
特价	Special offer(s)
打三折	30% off (by changing the number you change the percentage, for example, 打四折 means 40% off)
八折	20% discount (七折 means 30% discount)

Hotels and restaurants

饭店	Hotel; restaurant
宾馆	Hotel, guest house
酒店	Hotel
旅馆	Hotel (usually small)
请勿打扰	Please do not disturb
酒吧	Bar, pub
饭馆	Restaurant
酒家	Restaurant (not in a hotel)
餐厅	Restaurant, dining hall, canteen
肉类	Meat dishes
鱼类	Fish dishes
鸡、鸭类	Chicken and duck dishes
汤类	Soups
蔬菜	Vegetables
饮料	Drinks
冷饮	Cold drinks
热饮	Hot drinks
米饭	Rice
面食	Noodles and dumplings

Entertainment

电影院	Cinema
剧场	Theatre
音乐厅	Concert hall
音乐会	Concert
迪斯科	Disco
售票处	Ticket office
客满	Sold out
楼上	Upstairs
楼下	Downstairs
(27)排	Row (27)
双号	Even numbers
单号	Odd numbers

Services

公安局	Public security bureau
银行	Bank
邮(电)局	Post office
公用电话	Public phone
商务中心	Business centre (normally in a hotel)
问讯处	Information point
出租汽车(站)	Taxi (rank/bay)
火车站	Train station
公共汽车(站)	Bus (station)
地铁站	Underground (station)
候车室	Waiting room (at railway and coach stations)
候机室	Lounge (at airport)
机场费	Airport tax
行李检查	Baggage inspection
行李托运处	Baggage check-in

Hospital

医院	Hospital
门诊部	Outpatients department
急诊室	Accident and emergency
挂号处	Registration
药方	Prescription
药房	Pharmacy
服用方法	Dosage/Directions for use

Chinese–English vocabulary

We have listed the Chinese–English vocabulary under their radicals, using the order adopted in all dictionaries: one-stroke radicals occurring first, then two-stroke radicals, then three-stroke, and so on. The order in which, for example, the one-stroke radicals occur is also that adopted in most dictionaries.

We have listed the vocabulary under **words** (two or more characters), rather than single characters, except where they occur as such in the book.

Words with the same initial character are listed according to the number of strokes in the **second** character, i.e. the smaller the number of strokes in the second character, the earlier the word occurs. For example, (东)方 with four strokes occurs before (东)北 with five strokes, which in turn occurs before (东)南 with nine strokes.

You will see that 东 has a * after it. This is because radical indexes vary slightly between dictionaries and certain characters may appear under different radicals in different dictionaries; e.g. 东 may occur under 一 *horizontal line* in one dictionary but under 木 *wood/tree* in another. We have marked such characters with an asterisk and listed them under both possible radicals. We hope this will help rather than confuse you!

You should also remember that some radicals, such as 口, 目, 木, are not used in modern Chinese for the words for *mouth*, *eye*, *wood/tree* but act as the **radicals** of their modern-day equivalents, e.g. *mouth* is 嘴 *zuǐ* (not *kǒu*), *eye* is 眼 *yǎn* (not *mù*) and *tree* is 树 *shù* (not *mù*).

The number in the left-hand column indicates the number of strokes of a character excluding its radical. 'R' in the column represents a radical. In the case of radicals which are introduced in this book, the number in the right-hand column indicates the unit in which it first appears. MT1 stands for Mini-test 1, MT2 for Mini-test 2.

一画				
R	`、`			2
4	主	*zhǔ*	to take the initiative	9
	主席	*zhǔxí*	chair(man)	9
R	一	*yī*	one	2
	一般	*yìbān*	usually	7
1	二*	*èr*	two	4
	七	*qī*	seven	4
2	上	*shàng*	up, above	MT1
	上午	*shàngwǔ*	morning	MT1
	上班	*shàng bān*	to go to work	6
	上海	*Shànghǎi*	Shanghai	5
	下	*xià*	down, below	4
	下午	*xiàwǔ*	afternoon	MT1
	下降	*xiàjiàng*	to decline	10
	万	*wàn*	ten thousand	9
	… 万岁！	*wànsuì*	long live . . . !	9
	三	*sān*	three	3
	三文治	*sānwénzhì*	sandwich	8
3	元	*yuán*	unit of Chinese currency	8
	不*	*bù*	not, no	4
	不止	*bùzhǐ*	not only	10
	五	*wǔ*	five	4

	开车	*kāi chē*	to drive	4
	开会	*kāi huì*	to hold a meeting	5
	开往	*kāiwǎng*	(of a bus, train) to	6
4	平	*píng*	flat; peace; level	4
	东*	*dōng*	east	3
	东方	*dōngfāng*	the East; oriental	8
	东北	*dōngběi*	northeast	6
	东南	*dōngnán*	southeast	6
5	至	*zhì*	to	8
6	更(生)	*gēng(shēng)*	to regenerate	9
	更	*gèng*	even	10
	两	*liǎng*	two (of a kind)	5
	来*	*lái*	to come	6
7	画	*huà*	painting; stroke	8; 10
	画展	*huàzhǎn*	art exhibition	8
	事	*shì*	matter	10
	表	*biǎo*	form; table; watch	5
R	丨			2
3	书	*shū*	book	4
	书店	*shūdiàn*	bookshop	7
	书展	*shūzhǎn*	book fair	8
4	半	*bàn*	half	5
	北*	*běi*	north	5
	北京	*Běijīng*	Beijing	5

	北爱尔兰	*Běi'ài'ěrlán*	Northern Ireland	5
	申请	*shēnqǐng*	to apply; application	7
	出*口	*chǔkǒu*	exit	5
	出生（年月）	*chūshēng (niányuè)*	(year/month of) birth	8
	出租	*chūzū*	for rent; to rent out	6
	出租汽车	*chūzūqìchē*	taxi	6
R	**J**			2
1	九*	*jiǔ*	nine	4
2	及	*jí*	and	7
	川	*chuān*	river; another name for Sichuan Province	8
3	币	*bì*	currency	MT1
4	生	*shēng*	birth; raw	4
	生日	*shēngrì*	birthday	MT1
	生词	*shēngcí*	new word	4
	乐园	*lèyuán*	amusement park	8
5	舌	*shé*	tongue	2
	后*	*hòu*	rear, behind	3
6	我*	*wǒ*	I; me	3
	乱	*luàn*	chaotic, (to be) in disorder	MT2
11	粤	*yuè*	another name for Guangdong Province	8

R	乛			2
1	了	*le*	modal particle	9
R	𠃌			2
1	刁	*diāo*	tricky	3
2	习	*xí*	to practise	3
R	乙(乛乚)			2
1	九*	*jiǔ*	nine	4

二画

R	冫	*bīng*	ice	4
4	冰柜	*bīngguì*	freezer	MT2
	冰箱	*bīngxiāng*	refrigerator	6
5	冷	*lěng*	cold	9
8	准	*zhǔn*	to allow	7
	凌晨	*língchén*	early morning	MT2
R	亠		above	5
2	六	*liù*	six	4
3	市场	*shìchǎng*	market	8
4	产品	*chǎnpǐn*	product	8
6	京	*jīng*	capital; another name for Beijing	5; 8
8	高兴	*gāoxìng*	happy	9
	离开	*líkāi*	to leave	7
9	商	*shāng*	commerce	7
	商店	*shāngdiàn*	shop	7

	商城	*shāngchéng*	shopping centre	8
R	讠 (言)	*yán*	speech	2
2	订	*dìng*	to book; subscribe to	2
	讥	*jī*	to scorn	2
	认识	*rènshi*	to know, recognize	9
4	讽	*fěng*	to mock	3
5	词	*cí*	word	3
	词典	*cídiǎn*	dictionary	10
6	话	*huà*	speech	2
	诗	*shī*	poem	3
7	说	*shuō*	to speak	3
	说话	*shuō huà*	to speak/say something	4
8	请	*qǐng*	to invite; please	MT1
R	二*	*èr*	two	3
1	干	*gàn*	to do	3
1	于	*yú*	at, in	3
R	十	*shí*	ten	4
1	千	*qiān*	thousand	9
4	华	*huá*	China (old word)	4
	华语	*huáyǔ*	Chinese language	4
7	南	*nán*	south	6
	南方	*nánfāng*	the South	8
	南京	*Nánjīng*	Nanjing	6

	南美	*Nánměi*	South America	6
8	真	*zhēn*	real; really	9
R	厂	*chǎng*	factory	2
2	厅	*tīng*	hall	3
6	厕所	*cèsuǒ*	toilet	3
8	原来	*yuánlái*	it turns out to be	10
R	⺈			
3	在*	*zài*	at, in	6
4	有*	*yǒu*	to have	4
R	匚			
5	医院	*yīyuàn*	hospital	8
R	刂	*dāo*	knife	3
4	刘	*Liú*	a surname	5
	刚	*gāng*	just	3
5	别	*bié*	don't; other	3
6	刻	*kè*	a quarter (of an hour)	5
	刺	*cì*	to prick	3
	到	*dào*	to arrive	6
	到达	*dàodá*	to arrive; arrival	7
	刷	*shuā*	brush	3
	剁	*duò*	to chop	3
8	剧	*jù*	drama	8
10	割	*gē*	to cut	3
R	冖		crown	

3	写	*xiě*	to write	3
R	冂			
4	同	*tóng*	same	8
R	宀			
2	午	*wǔ*	noon	MT1
	午餐	*wǔcān*	lunch	MT2
4	年	*nián*	year	4
	年年	*niánnián*	every year	4
R	亻	*rén*	person	2
2	仍	*réng*	still	10
3	们	*men*	plural for person	2
	他	*tā*	he; him	4
	代代	*dàidài*	every generation	4
4	休	*xiū*	to rest	2
	伦敦	*Lúndūn*	London	9
5	伴	*bàn*	companion	2
	住	*zhù*	to live/stay	6
	你	*nǐ*	you (singular)	6
	低	*dī*	low	9
	位于	*wèiyú*	to be situated at/in	MT2
6	例外	*lìwài*	exception	10
7	保险室	*bǎoxiǎnshì*	deposit box(es)	5
	信	*xìn*	letter	2
	信用卡	*xìnyòngkǎ*	credit card	7

8	健康	*jiànkāng*	healthy	9
9	停车	*tíng chē*	to stop/park a vehicle	6
R	厂			2
4	后*	*hòu*	rear, behind	3
R	人; 入	*rén; rù*	person; to enter	1; 3
	人人	*rénrén*	everybody	4
	人口	*rénkǒu*	population	4
	入口	*rùkǒu*	entry	4
	人民	*rénmín*	the people (of a country)	MT1
	人民币	*Rénmínbì*	*renminbi* (Chinese currency)	MT1
	人民日报	*Rénmín Rìbào*	*the People's Daily* (newspaper)	MT1
	人民大会堂	*Rénmín Dàhuìtáng*	the Great Hall of the People	MT1
	人所周知	*rén suǒ zhōu zhī*	it is known to everyone	10
	入场	*rùchǎng*	entrance, admission	8
2	今(日)	*jīn(rì)*	today	8
	以上	*yǐshàng*	over, more than	10
4	会	*huì*	meeting	5
	会	*huì*	will (showing possibility)	9
	会谈	*huìtán*	talk; negotiation	9
	众	*zhòng*	crowd	2

8	拿*	*ná*	to take	10
R	八(丷)	*bā*	eight	4
2	分	*fēn*	minute; the smallest unit of Chinese currency	5
	公	*gōng*	public	4
	公斤	*gōngjīn*	kilogram	8
	公平	*gōngpíng*	fair, just	4
	公司	*gōngsī*	company	7
	公园	*gōngyuán*	park	4
	公里	*gōnglǐ*	kilometre	8
	公共	*gōnggòng*	public	6
	公共汽车	*gōnggòng qìchē*	bus	6
	公道	*gōngdào*	public road; justice	7
	公路	*gōnglù*	public road	8
5	弟弟	*dìdi*	younger brother	5
	谷	*gǔ*	valley	8
6	单	*dān*	single	8
	单号	*dānhào*	odd number	8
7	差*	*chà*	to lack; poor (in quality)	5
	前	*qián*	front	7
R	勹			2
2	勿	*wù*	not, no	6

R	刀 (⺀)	dāo	knife	3
5	免费	miǎnfèi	free of charge	8
	免税	miǎn shuì	duty-free	6
R	力	lì	strength	2
2	办公室	bàngōngshì	office	5
3	加拿大	Jiānádà	Canada	5
R	儿	ér	child	7
	儿童	értóng	child, children	7
R	卩			
3	印象派	yìnxiàngpài	impressionist	8
R	阝 (LHS)		mound	5
4	阴	yīn	cloudy	9
5	陈	Chén	a surname	5
7	除	chú	to get rid of	MT2
9	随地	suídì	at any place	6
R	阝 (RHS)		town, region	5
5	邮票	yóupiào	stamp	7
	邮(电)局	yóu(diàn)jú	post office	5
6	郑	Zhèng	a surname	5
8	郭	Guō	a surname	5
	都	dōu	all	6
R	又	yòu	again	5
2	双	shuāng	double	8
	双号	shuānghào	even numbers	8

	欢迎	*huānyíng*	welcome	5
8	难	*nán*	difficult	4
	难吃	*nánchī*	awful to eat	4
	难听	*nántīng*	unpleasant to listen to	4
	难看	*nánkàn*	ugly	4
R	厶			2
3	台湾	*Táiwān*	Taiwan	5
	参观	*cānguān*	to visit, visit	5
R	匕	*bǐ*	stagger	
3	北*	*běi*	north	5
	北京	*Běijīng*	Beijing	5
	北海	*Běihǎi*	North Sea	5

三画

R	氵	*shuǐ*	water	2
2	汉字	*hànzì*	Chinese character	4
3	江	*jiāng*	river	2
	汗	*hàn*	sweat	2
	污	*wū*	dirty	MT2
4	沪	*hù*	another name for Shanghai	8
	汽车	*qìchē*	vehicle	6
5	法(律)	*fǎ(lù)*	law	5, 10
	法国	*Fǎguó*	France	5
	河	*hé*	river	3

	河南	*Hénán*	Henan Province	6
	河北	*Héběi*	Hebei Province	6
	泪	*lèi*	tear (when crying)	2
6	洋	*yáng*	ocean	7
	津	*jīn*	another name for Tianjin	8
7	酒	*jiǔ*	alcohol	5
	酒吧	*jiǔbā*	bar, pub	5
	酒店	*jiǔdiàn*	hotel	7
	海	*hǎi*	sea	3
	海南	*Hǎinán*	Hainan Province	6
8	清	*qīng*	clear; Qing Dynasty	MT1; 9
9	湖	*hú*	lake	6
	湖北	*Húběi*	Hubei Province	6
	湖南	*Húnán*	Hunan Province	6
	港	*gǎng*	harbour; another name for Hong Kong	8
	湘	*Xiāng*	another name for Hunan Province	8
12	潮	*cháo*	tide	7
R	忄	*xīn*	heart	2
3	忙	*máng*	busy	9
4	快乐	*kuàilè*	happy	9
5	怕	*pà*	to fear	2

	性别	*xìngbié*	sex, gender	8
6	恨	*hèn*	to hate	2
8	情	*qíng*	feeling	MT1
R	广	*guǎng*	broad	3, 5
	广东	*Guǎngdōng*	Guangdong Province	5
	广西	*Guǎngxī*	Guangxi Autonomous Region	6
	广场	*guǎngchǎng*	square	MT1
5	店	*diàn*	shop	7
	店员	*diànyuán*	shop assistant	5
7	座	*zuò*	seat	7
	席	*xí*	mat, seat	9
R	宀		roof	2
3	安	*ān*	peace	2
	字	*zì*	Chinese character	4
4	灾	*zāi*	disaster	2
5	宝玉	*bǎoyù*	precious jade	8
6	客(人)	*kè(rén)*	guest	7
	客满	*kèmǎn*	sold out	8
	室	*shì*	room	7
7	家	*jiā*	home, family	2
8	寄	*jì*	to post/mail a letter, etc.	7
	寄件人	*jìjiànrén*	sender	7

R	门	*mén*	door	4
4	间	*jiān*	during	10
R	辶		to walk (quickly)	2
3	迈	*mài*	to step over	2
	过	*guò*	to pass	2
4	还	*hái*	still	10
	远	*yuǎn*	far	2
	近	*jìn*	close, near	10
	这儿，这里	*zhèr, zhèlǐ*	here	4, 9
6	逃	*táo*	to escape	2
	送餐	*sòng cān*	food delivery	7
R	工	*gōng*	work	2
	工人	*gōngrén*	worker	4
	工作	*gōngzuò*	work, to work	9
	工作单位	*gōngzuò dānwèi*	work unit	8
R	土	*tǔ*	earth	2
2	去	*qù*	to go	6
3	在*	*zài*	at, in	6
	尘*	*chén*	dust	3
	场	*chǎng*	square; open space	8
	地址	*dìzhǐ*	address	7
	地点	*dìdiǎn*	venue	8
	地中海	*Dìzhōnghǎi*	the Mediterranean	6

4	坐	*zuò*	to sit	2
6	城(市)	*chéng(shì)*	town, city	9, (7)
9	喜*欢	*xǐhuān*	to like	6
11	墙	*qiáng*	wall	2
R	⺿	*cǎo*	grass	
4	花	*huā*	flower	2
	花园	*huāyuán*	garden	4
	芽	*yá*	sprout	2
	苏格兰	*Sūgélán*	Scotland	5
5	英	*yīng*	hero	5
	英文	*Yīngwén*	English language	8
	英里	*yīnglǐ*	mile	8
	英国	*Yīngguó*	Britain (often used for England)	5
	英语	*Yīngyǔ*	English language	10
	英格兰	*Yīnggélán*	England	5
6	草	*cǎo*	grass	2
	茶	*chá*	tea	5
7	莫	*mò*	do not	9
8	菜	*cài*	vegetable; dish	8
	营业	*yíngyè*	business	MT2
	黄	*huáng*	yellow	7
9	葡萄酒	*pútáojiǔ*	wine	5
14	藏	*Zàng*	Zang nationality; Tibetan	6

R	大	*dà*	big	2
	大人	*dàrén*	adult	4
	大学	*dàxué*	university	4
1	太平洋	*Tàipíngyáng*	the Pacific Ocean	7
R	寸	*cùn*	unit of length (= 1/30 metre)	5
R	扌	*shǒu*	hand	2
2	打	*dǎ*	to hit	2
	扔	*rēng*	to throw	2
3	扣	*kòu*	(to) button	3
	扬子江	*Yángzijiāng*	the Yangtze River	7
4	找	*zhǎo*	to look for	3
	报	*bào*	newspaper	9
	护照	*hùzhào*	passport	7
5	拥	*yōng*	to possess	9
	拌	*bàn*	to blend	2
8	推	*tuī*	to push	3
	排	*pái*	row	7
	接收人	*jiēshōurén*	recipient (of a letter)	7
R	弋			
2	式	*shì*	style, form	7
R	巾	*jīn*	towel, napkin	5
R	口	*kǒu*	mouth	2
	口香糖	*kǒuxiāngtáng*	chewing gum	MT2

2	只	*zhǐ*	only	7
	叮	*dīng*	to sting	3
	号	*hào*	number; date	7; 9
	号码	*hàomǎ*	number	7
	可是	*kěshì*	but	9
	可口可乐	*kěkǒukělè*	Coca-Cola	5
3	吃	*chī*	to eat	3
	吃饭	*chī fàn*	to eat (something)	4
	吸	*xī*	to breathe in	3
	吸烟	*xī yān*	to smoke	6
	吐痰	*tù tán*	to spit	6
4	吴	*Wú*	a surname	5
	吻	*wěn*	kiss, to kiss	2
	员	*yuán*	person (in a trade)	5
	听	*tīng*	to listen	4
	听见	*tīngjiàn*	to hear	4
	听说	*tīngshuō*	to hear someone say	4
	听懂	*tīngdǒng*	to understand	4
	君	*jūn*	gentleman (classical Chinese)	MT2
5	咖啡	*kāfēi*	coffee	5
	咖啡馆	*kāfēiguǎn*	café	6
6	品	*pǐn*	product	7
	哪知道 …?	*nǎ zhīdao . . . ?*	who would have thought . . . ?	10

7	哥哥	*gēge*	elder brother	5
8	唯一	*wéiyī*	only	7
9	喝	*hē*	to drink	3
	喜*欢	*xǐhuan*	to like	6
	啤酒	*píjiǔ*	beer	5
13	器	*qì*	appliance	7
R	囗		enclosure	2
2	囚	*qiú*	prisoner	2
	四	*sì*	four	4
	四川	*Sìchuān*	Sichuan Province	5
3	回	*huí*	to return	6
4	园	*yuán*	garden	2
5	国	*guó*	country, state	3
	国内	*guónèi*	(of a country) domestic	10
	国际	*guójì*	international	7
	国语	*guóyǔ*	national language	4
	图书展销会	*túshū zhǎnxiāohuì*	book fair	8
7	圆	*yuán*	unit of Chinese currency	8
R	山	*shān*	mountain	1
	山东	*Shāndōng*	Shandong Province	6
	山西	*Shānxī*	Shanxi Province	6
4	岗	*gǎng*	hillock	3

5	岭	*lǐng*	hill	3
7	峰	*fēng*	peak	3
8	崖	*yá*	cliff	3
R	彳		step with left foot	3
3	行李	*xínglǐ*	luggage	7
6	很	*hěn*	very	6
9	街	*jiē*	street	8
12	德	*dé*	virtue	5
	德国	*Déguó*	Germany	5
R	夕			
3	名	*míng*	(given) name	7
	多	*duō*	many, much	9
R	夂			
2	处	*chù*	place	7
5	备注	*bèizhù*	remark	7
R	尸	*shī*	corpse	
4	局	*jú*	bureau	7
7	展览馆	*zhǎnlǎnguǎn*	exhibition hall	8
	展销会	*zhǎnxiāohuì*	trade fair	8
R	饣	*shí*	food	3
4	饭	*fàn*	food	3
	饭店	*fàndiàn*	restaurant; hotel	5
	饭馆	*fànguǎn*	restaurant	6
	饮料	*yǐnliào*	drinks	5

5	饱	*bǎo*	to be full up	3
6	饼	*bǐng*	pancake	3
	饺	*jiǎo*	dumpling	3
7	饿	*è*	hungry	3
8	馅	*xiàn*	stuffing	3
R	犭	*quǎn*	(wild) animal	3
5	狗	*gǒu*	dog	3
	狐	*hú*	fox	3
6	独立	*dúlì*	independent	9
7	狼	*láng*	wolf	3
8	猫	*māo*	cat	3
R	彐			
5	录音	*lù yīn*	to record	4
R	弓	*gōng*	bow	
4	张	*Zhāng*	a surname	5
R	己; 已	*jǐ; yǐ*	self; already	3
	已经	*yǐjīng*	already	9
R	女	*nǚ*	female	2
	女厕所	*nǚ cèsuǒ*	women's toilets	5
2	奴	*nú*	slave	6
3	她	*tā*	she; her	2
	奸	*jiān*	to rape	6
	好	*hǎo*	good	2
	好吃	*hǎochī*	delicious	4

	好心	*hǎoxīn*	kind-hearted	4
	好听	*hǎotīng*	pleasant to listen to	4
	好看	*hǎokàn*	good-looking	4
	妈妈	*māma*	mum, mother	5
	如意	*rúyì*	as one wishes	9
5	姓	*xìng*	surname	7
	姓名	*xìngmíng*	name	7
	妹妹	*mèimei*	younger sister	5
	姐姐	*jiějie*	elder sister	5
8	娶	*qǔ*	to marry (of a man)	6
10	嫁	*jià*	to marry (of a woman)	6
R	子	*zǐ*	child	1
5	学(习)	*xué(xí)*	to learn, to study; study	3; (4)
	学院	*xuéyuàn*	college, institute	8
R	马	*mǎ*	horse	1
4	驴	*lǘ*	donkey	2
5	驹	*jū*	pony	2
8	骑	*qí*	to ride	2
11	骡	*luó*	mule	2
R	纟	*sī*	silk	4
3	级	*jí*	grade	9
	红	*hóng*	red	8
5	线	*xiàn*	line, thread	8

6	统计	*tǒngjì*	statistics	10
8	绿	*lǜ*	green	8
R	小 (⺌)	*xiǎo*	small	2
	小人	*xiǎo rén*	small-minded person	4
	小心	*xiǎo xīn*	careful	4
	小吃	*xiǎochī*	snack	8
	小时	*xiǎoshí*	hour	7
	小学	*xiǎoxué*	primary school	4
	小费	*xiǎofèi*	tip, gratuity	4
3	尖	*jiān*	sharp	2
	尘*	*chén*	dust	3
	当	*dāng*	to act/serve as	3
	光临	*guānglín*	to be present	8
8	常常	*chángcháng*	often	9

四画

R	灬	*huǒ*	fire	2
5	点	*diǎn*	o'clock	5
6	热	*rè*	hot	9
8	煮	*zhǔ*	to boil	3
9	照相	*zhào xiàng*	to take a photo	6
R	心	*xīn*	heart	2
4	念书	*niàn shū*	to study	4
9	想	*xiǎng*	to think; to miss somebody	2

182

	意*大利	*Yìdàlì*	Italy	5
R	火	*huǒ*	fire	2
	火山	*huǒshān*	volcano	MT1
	火车	*huǒchē*	train	4
	火花	*huǒhuā*	spark	MT1
	火腿	*huǒtuǐ*	ham	MT1
	火箭	*huǒjiàn*	rocket	MT1
3	灶	*zào*	stove	2
4	炎	*yán*	burning hot	2
6	烧	*shāo*	to burn	3
8	焱	*yàn*	flame	2
R	文	*wén*	writing, literature	MT2
	文物	*wénwù*	cultural object(s)	MT2
2	刘	*Liú*	a surname	5
R	方	*fāng*	square	5
4	放心	*fàng xīn*	to be at ease	4
6	旅	*lǚ*	to travel	10
	旅行(社)	*lǚxíng(shè)*	travel (agency)	7
	旅游	*lǚyóu*	to travel, travel	7
R	户	*hù*	household	2
4	房	*fáng*	house	2
	房号	*fáng hào*	room number	7
	房间	*fángjiān*	room	7
R	礻		omen; to express	5

5	祝	*zhù*	to wish	9
	祝贺	*zhùhè*	to congratulate	10
R	王	*Wáng*	a surname; king	4
	王子	*wángzi*	prince	4
4	现在	*xiànzài*	now, present	9
	现住址	*xiànzhùzhǐ*	present address	8
5	珍惜	*zhēnxī*	to treasure	9
R	天	*tiān*	day, heaven	4
	天子	*tiānzi*	emperor (son of heaven)	4
	天天	*tiāntiān*	every day	4
	天气	*tiānqì*	weather	4
	天气预报	*tiānqìyùbào*	weather forecast	9
	天地	*tiāndì*	heaven and earth	8
	天津	*Tiānjīn*	Tianjin	8
R	木	*mù*	wood	1
	木工	*mùgōng*	carpenter	4
2	东*	*dōng*	east	3
	杂	*zá*	mixed	3
	乐园	*lèyuán*	paradise	8
3	李	*Lǐ*	a surname	5
	村	*cūn*	village	2
	材	*cái*	timber	3
4	林	*lín*	wood; a surname	2

	枫	*fēng*	maple	3
6	根	*gēn*	root	3
	根据	*gēnjù*	according to	10
7	检字表	*jiǎnzìbiǎo*	character index	10
8	森(林)	*sēn(lín)*	forest	2, (5)
	椅	*yǐ*	chair	2
9	楼	*lóu*	building, house	5
	楼上	*lóushàng*	upstairs	6
	楼下	*lóuxià*	downstairs	8
	楼梯	*lóutī*	stairs	5
R	不*	*bù*	not, no	4
	不止	*bùzhǐ*	not only	10
3	否	*fǒu*	not; no; deny; or not	6
5	歪	*wāi*	crooked	6
	甭	*béng*	don't	6
6	孬	*nāo*	bad	6
R	车	*chē*	vehicle	1
	车次	*chēcì*	train number	MT2
	车道	*chēdào*	vehicle lane	7
R	戈	*gē*	spear	
	威尔士	*Wēi'ěrshì*	Wales	5
3	我*	*wǒ*	I; me	6
R	止	*zhǐ*	to stop, to end	
1	正宗	*zhèngzōng*	(of food) authentic	MT2

2	此刻	*cǐkè*	at this moment	10
R	日	*rì*	sun, day	1
	日历	*rìlì*	calendar	MT1
	日出	*rìchū*	sunrise	5
	日本	*Rìběn*	Japan	5
	日航	*Rìháng*	Japan Airlines	7
	日期	*rìqī*	date	7
	日程表	*rìchéngbiǎo*	itinerary, programme	5
2	早	*zǎo*	early	MT1
	早上	*zǎoshang*	early morning	4
	早安	*zǎo'ān*	Good morning!	MT1
	早饭	*zǎofàn*	breakfast	6
	早晨	*zǎochén*	early morning	9
	早餐	*zǎocān*	breakfast	7
3	时(间)	*shí(jiān)*	time	3, (7)
4	明	*míng*	bright	2
	明天	*míngtiān*	tomorrow	4
5	昨(天)	*zuó(tiān)*	yesterday	3, (9)
	星(星)	*xīng(xīng)*	star	4, (8)
	星期	*xīngqī*	week	4
6	晃	*huǎng*	to dazzle	3
7	晚	*wǎn*	evening; late	3, MT1
	晚上	*wǎnshang*	evening	4
	晚餐	*wǎncān*	dinner	MT2

8	晴	*qíng*	bright, sunny	MT1
	普通话	*Pǔtōnghuà*	Modern Standard Chinese	4
9	暖	*nuǎn*	warm	2
R	曰	*yuē*	to say (classical Chinese)	
1	电*	*diàn*	electricity, electric	4
	电车	*diànchē*	tram	4
	电台	*diàntái*	radio station	5
	电话	*diànhuà*	telephone	4
	电脑	*diànnǎo*	computer	4
	电视	*diànshì*	television	4
	电梯	*diàntī*	lift, elevator	5
	电影	*diànyǐng*	film	4
	电影院	*diànyǐngyuàn*	cinema	7
	电器	*diànqì*	electric appliance(s)	7
8	最	*zuì*	the most	9
R	中*	*zhōng*	middle, centre	5
	中心	*zhōngxīn*	centre; heart	MT1
	中午	*zhōngwǔ*	noon	MT1
	中东	*Zhōngdōng*	the Middle East	6
	中学	*zhōngxué*	secondary/high school	MT1
	中国	*Zhōngguó*	China	MT1
R	贝	*bèi*	shell	3

3	贡	*gòng*	tribute	3
4	货	*huò*	goods	3
5	贵	*guì*	expensive	3
	费	*fèi*	fee(s)	4
	贴	*tiē*	to stick on	7
	贺	*hè*	to congratulate	10
6	资	*zī*	capital; money	3
R	见	*jiàn*	to see	3
R	父	*fù*	father	5
4	爸爸	*bàba*	dad, father	5
R	气	*qì*	air	4
	气温	*qìwēn*	(weather) temperature	9
6	氧	*yǎng*	oxygen	10
8	氰	*qíng*	cyanogen	MT1
R	牛	*niú*	cattle, cow	3
4	物	*wù*	object, thing	10
R	手	*shǒu*	hand	2
6	拿*	*ná*	to take	10
R	毛	*máo*	fur, hair	2
R	攵		to tap, rap	5
2	收	*shōu*	to receive	7
	收件人	*shōujiànrén*	recipient (of a letter, etc.)	7
7	教书	*jiāo shū*	to teach	4

	教育展	*jiàoyù(zhǎn)*	education (exhibition)	8
8	数字	*shùzì*	number	10
R	斤	*jīn*	half a kilogram	8
9	新	*xīn*	new	7
R	爪(爫)	*zhǎo, zhuǎ*	claws	
6	爱(愛)	*ài*	to love, love	2
	爱尔兰	*Ài'ěrlán*	Ireland	5
R	尺	*chǐ*	$\frac{1}{3}$ of a metre	8
R	月	*yuè*	moon; flesh	1
	月月	*yuèyuè*	every month	4
	月票	*yuèpiào*	monthly (travel) pass	4
4	朋友	*péngyou*	friend	9
	服务	*fúwù*	service, to serve	5
	服务台	*fúwùtái*	reception	5
	服务员	*fúwùyuán*	attendant	5
	服务楼	*fúwùlóu*	service block	5
R	风	*fēng*	wind	4
	风力	*fēnglì*	wind force	9
	风水	*fēngshuǐ*	fengshui	4
	风向	*fēngxiàng*	wind direction	9
	风味	*fēngwèi*	style of cooking	5
R	比	*bǐ*	to compare	10
R	水	*shuǐ*	water	4
	水准	*shuǐzhǔn*	level, standard	10

五画

R	立	*lì*	to stand	5
5	站	*zhàn*	station; stop (bus etc.)	6
	站台	*zhàntái*	platform	MT2
R	病(疒)	*bìng*	illness	5
R	衤(衣)	*yī*	clothes	4
R	穴	*xué*	cave	4
R	玉	*yù*	jade	5
R	示	*shì*	to show	5
8	禁止	*jìnzhǐ*	to prohibit	6
R	石	*shí*	stone, mineral	2
3	矿泉水	*kuàngquánshuǐ*	mineral water	5
	码	*mǎ*	number	8
7	确认	*quèrèn*	to confirm	7
8	碗	*wǎn*	bowl	2
10	磅	*bàng*	pound (weight)	8
R	戍	*shù*	to defend	
1	成功	*chénggōng*	success; successful	9
	成语	*chéngyǔ*	idiom, proverb	10
R	业			
6	常*常	*chángcháng*	often	9
R	目	*mù*	eye	2
	目的地	*mùdìdì*	destination	7

190

2	盯	*dīng*	to stare	3
3	眨	*zhǎ*	to blink	3
4	看	*kàn*	to look at; to watch	4
	看见	*kànjiàn*	to see	4
	看懂	*kàndǒng*	to understand	4
6	眼	*yǎn*	eye	3
10	瞎	*xiā*	blind	3
	瞎话	*xiāhuà*	lie	4
R	田	*tián*	field	2
2	男	*nán*	male	2
	男厕所	*náncèsuǒ*	men's toilets	5
R	皿			
3	罗马	*Luómǎ*	Rome	MT2
R	钅	*jīn*	metal	2
2	钉	*dīng*	nail, to nail	2
4	钢	*gāng*	steel	2
	钟	*zhōng*	clock	5
5	铃	*líng*	bell	2
	钱	*qián*	money	4
6	银行	*yínháng*	bank	5
7	锈	*xiù*	rust; to rust	2
R	矢	*shǐ*	arrow	
3	知道	*zhīdào*	to know (a fact)	10
R	禾	*hé*	plant; grain	4

3	和平	*hépíng*	peace	9
4	香港	*Xiānggǎng*	Hong Kong	5
R	白	*bái*	white	
1	百	*bǎi*	hundred	9
3	的	*de*	*particle*	6
R	鸟	*niǎo*	bird (long-tailed)	5
2	鸡	*jī*	chicken	
R	癶			
	登机门	*dēng jīmén*	boarding gate	8
六画				
R	羊	*yáng*	sheep	2
3	差*	*chà*	to lack; poor (in quality)	5
	美	*měi*	beautiful	5
	美术(馆)	*měishù(guǎn)*	art (gallery)	8
	美国	*Měiguó*	America	5
R	米	*mǐ*	rice (uncooked); metre	3; 8
	米饭	*mǐfàn*	cooked rice	6
R	衣 (衤)	*yī*	clothes	4
R	西	*xī*	west	6
	西北	*xīběi*	northwest	6
	西汉	*Xīhàn*	West Han (Dynasty)	9
	西安	*Xī'ān*	Xi'an	6
	西南	*xīnán*	southwest	6

	西晋	*Xījìn*	West Jin (Dynasty)	9
	西藏	*Xīzàng*	Tibet	6
3	要	*yào*	to want	8
5	票（价）	*piào(jià)*	ticket (price)	8
R	页	*yè*	page	3
R	虫	*chóng*	insect	4
8	蜻（蜓）	*qīng(tíng)*	dragonfly	MT1
R	舌	*shé*	tongue	2
R	竹 (⺮)	*zhú*	bamboo	2
4	笔	*bǐ*	(brush) pen	2
5	第	*dì*	(for ordinal number)	4
7	签名	*qiānmíng*	to sign; signature	7
R	自	*zì*	self	9
	自主	*zìzhǔ*	self-determination	9
R	舟	*zhōu*	boat	
4	航空	*hángkōng*	by air	7
	航班	*hángbān*	flight	7

七画

R	言(讠)	*yán*	speech	2
R	走	*zǒu*	to go, walk	4
	走路	*zǒu lù*	to walk	4
2	赵	*Zhào*	a surname	5
3	起飞	*qǐfēi*	to take off	7
5	越南	*Yuènán*	Vietnam	5

R	酉	*yǒu*	spirit made from ripe millet; Tenth of Twelve Earthly Branches	5
R	豕	*shǐ*	pig	2
R	足	*zú*	foot	5
6	路	*lù*	road, street	4
R	身	*shěn*	body	
	身体	*shěntǐ*	body; health	9
R	角	*jiǎo*	horn; unit of Chinese currency, $\frac{1}{10}$ of one *yuan*	8
6	触电	*chùdiàn*	electric shock	6
八画以上				
R	青	*qīng*	green; another name for Qinghai Province	8
	青海	*Qīnghǎi*	Qinghai Province	8
R	雨	*yǔ*	rain	1
3	雪	*xuě*	snow	2
5	零	*líng*	zero	4
R	鱼	*yú*	fish	1
4	鲁	*Lǔ*	another name for Shangdong Province	8
6	鲜	*xiān*	fresh	2
8	鲭	*qīng*	mackerel	MT1

R	音	*yīn*	sound	4
4	意*大利	*Yìdàlì*	Italy	5
R	食	*shí*	food	3
	食品	*shípǐn*	food (product)	7
7	餐厅	*cāntīng*	dining hall, restaurant	5
Other				
	卡片	*kǎpiàn*	card	4
	巴士	*bāshi* (pidgin English)	bus	6

English–Chinese vocabulary

This vocabulary list includes only the most significant words that have occurred in this course. Numbers in the right-hand column are unit numbers.

address	地址	7
admission, entrance	入内	8
adult	大人	4
afternoon	下午	MT1
air	气	4
alcohol	酒	5
to allow	准	7
America	美国	5
to apply; application	申请	7
to arrive	到	6
to arrive; arrival	到达	7
at, in	在	6
attendant	服务员	5
awful (to eat)	难吃	4
bank	银行	5
bar, pub	酒吧	5
beautiful	美	5
beer	啤酒	5
Beijing	北京	5
big	大	2
bird	鸟	5
birthday	生日	MT1
body; health	身体	9
to boil	煮	3
Bon voyage!	一路平安！	9
book	书	4
to book; subscribe to	订	2
book fair	图书展销会	8
bookshop	书店	7

bowl	碗	2
breakfast	早饭, 早餐	6, 7
to breathe in	吸	3
Britain, England	英国	5
building, house	楼	5
to burn	烧	3
bus	公共汽车	6
business	营业	MT2
busy	忙	9
but	可是	9
by air	航空	7
café	咖啡馆	6
calendar	日历	MT1
Canada	加拿大	5
card	卡(片)	4
careful	小心	4
cat	猫	3
cattle, cow	牛	3
centre	中心	MT1
chicken	鸡	8
child, children	儿童	7
China	中国	MT1
Chinese (Modern Standard)	普通话	4
Chinese character	字, 汉字	3
cinema	电影院	7
clock	钟	5
close, near	近	10
clothes	衣(服)	4
cloudy	阴	9
Coca-Cola	可口可乐	5
cold	冷	9
college, institute	学院	8
to come	来	6
commerce	商	7
company	公司	7
to compare	比	10
computer	电脑	4
to congratulate	祝贺	10

fair, just	公平	4
far	远	2
father	爸爸	5
to fear	怕	2
fee(s)	费	7
female	女	2
fengshui	风水	4
field	田	2
film	电影	4
fire	火	2
fish	鱼	1
five	五	4
flower	花	2
food (product)	食品	7
four	四	4
France	法国	5
free of charge	免费	8
freezer	冰柜	MT2
friend	朋友	9
fur, hair	毛	2
garden	花园	4
gender, sex	性别	8
Germany	德国	5
to go	去	6
to go to work	上班	6
good	好	2
good-looking	好看	4
Good luck!	祝你走运!	9
Good morning!	早安!	MT1
green	绿	8
guest	客	7
half	半	5
half a kilogram	斤	8
ham	火腿	MT1
hand	手	2
happy	高兴, 快乐	9
Happy birthday!	生日快乐!	9

Happy (Chinese) New Year!	春节快乐!	9
Happy Christmas!	圣诞节快乐!	9
Happy Easter!	复活节快乐!	9
Happy New Year!	新年快乐!	9
Happy Valentine's Day!	情人节快乐!	9
to hate	恨	2
to have	有	4
he; him	他	4
health	身体	9
healthy	健康	9
to hear	听见	4
heart	心	2
to hit	打	2
to hold a meeting	开会	5
home, family	家	2
Hong Kong	香港	5
horse	马	1
hospital	医院	8
hot	热	9
hotel, restaurant	饭店, 酒店	4, 7
hour	小时	7
hundred	百	9
hungry	饿	3
I; me	我	6
idiom, proverb	成语	10
illness	病	5
international	国际	7
to invite; please	请	MT1
Italy	意大利	5
itinerary, programme	日程表	5
Japan	日本	5
jiao (unit of Chinese currency, $\frac{1}{10}$ of one *yuan*)	角	8
kilogram	公斤	8
kilometre	公里	8
kiss, to kiss	吻	2
knife	刀	3

to know (a fact)	知道	10
to know, recognize	认识	9
to lack; poor (in quality)	差	5
lake	湖	6
law	法(律)	5, 10
to leave	离开	7
letter	信	2
level, standard	水准	10
lie	瞎话	4
lift, elevator	电梯	5
to like	喜欢	6
to listen	听	4
London	伦敦	8
long live . . . !	… 万岁!	9
to look at; to watch	看	4
to look for	找	3
love, to love	爱(爱)	2
luggage/baggage	行李	7
lunch	午餐	9
to mail (a letter, etc.)	寄	7
male	男	2
many, much	多	9
market	市场	8
the Mediterranean	地中海	6
men's toilets	男厕所	5
middle, centre	中	5
the Middle East	中东	6
mile	英里	8
mineral water	矿泉水	5
minute; the smallest unit of Chinese currency	分	5
money	钱	4
moon	月	1
morning	上午	MT1
the most	最	9
mountain	山	1
mum, mother	妈妈	5

name	姓名	7
Nanjing	南京	6
near	近	10
new	新	7
new word	生词	4
newspaper	报	9
nine	九	4
noon	中午	MT1
north	北	5
northeast	东北	6
northwest	西北	6
not, no	不	4
now, present	现在	9
number (room, telephone, etc.)	号; 号码	7
number	数字	10
object, thing	物	10
o'clock	点	5
odd number	单号	8
office	办公室	5
often	常常	9
one	一	2
oriental; (the) East	东方	6, 8
Pacific Ocean	太平洋	7
page	页	3
painting	画	8
park	公园	4
to pass	过	2
passport	护照	7
peace	和平	9
pen (brush)	笔	2
(the) people	人民	MT1
person	人	1
platform	站台	MT2
pleasant to listen to	好听	4
population	人口	4
to post, mail	寄	7
post office	邮(电)局	5

primary school	小学	4
product	产品	8
to prohibit	禁止	6
pub	酒吧	5
public	公共	6
public road	公路	8
to push	推	3
quarter (of an hour)	刻	5
radio station	电台	5
rain	雨	1
to read books, to study	念书	4
real; really	真	9
rear, behind	后	3
reception	服务台	5
to record	录音	4
red	红	8
refrigerator	冰箱	6
renminbi (Chinese currency)	人民币	MT1
to rent out; for rent	出租	6
restaurant	饭馆	6
restaurant, hotel	饭店	5
to return	回	9
to ride	骑	2
river	河	3
road, street	路	4
room	房间	7
room number	房号	7
row	排	7
sea	海	3
secondary/high school	中学	MT1
to see	看见	4
to send a letter, etc.	寄	7
service, to serve	服务	5
seven	七	4
sex, gender	性别	8
Shanghai	上海	5
she; her	她	2

sheep	羊	2
shop	商店	7
shopping centre	商城	8
to sign; signature	签名	7
to sit	坐	2
six	六	4
slave	奴	6
small	小	2
to smoke	吸烟	6
snack	小吃	8
snow	雪	2
sold out	客满	8
south	南	6
South America	南美	6
southeast	东南	6
southwest	西南	6
to speak	说(话)	4
stairs	楼梯	5
stamp (postage)	邮票	7
statistics	统计	10
to stick on	贴	7
to stop/park a vehicle	停车	6
street	街	8
stroke	画	8
study, to study	学习	4
success(ful)	成功	9
sunny, bright	晴	4
sunrise	日出	5
surname	姓	7
to take	拿	10
to take a photo	照相	6
talks; negotiations	会谈	9
taxi	出租汽车	6
tea	茶	5
to teach	教书	4
tear (when crying)	泪	2
telephone	电话	4
television	电视	4

temperature (weather)	气温	9
ten	十	4
ten thousand	万	9
to think; to miss somebody	想	2
thousand	千	9
three	三	4
Tianjin	天津	8
Tibet	西藏	6
ticket price	票价	8
time	时(间)	3, (7)
tip, gratuity	小费	4
to (of a bus, train)	开往	6
toilet	厕所	3
tomorrow	明天	4
town, city	城(市)	9, (7)
trade fair	展销会	8
train	火车	4
train number	车次	MT2
tram	电车	4
travel (agency)	旅行(社)	7
travel, to travel	旅游	7
two	二	4
two (of a kind)	两	5
ugly	难看	4
to understand	(听/看)懂	4
university	大学	4
unpleasant to listen to	难听	4
up, above	上	MT1
upstairs	楼上	6
vegetable; dish	菜	8
vehicle	车, 汽车	1, 6
venue	地点	8
very	很	6
visit, to visit	参观	5
to walk	走(路)	4
to want	要	8
warm	暖	2

water	水	4
weather	天气	4
weather forecast	天气预报	9
week	星期	4
welcome, to welcome	欢迎	5
west	西	6
(the) West	西方	6
wind	风	4
windy	有风	9
wine	葡萄酒	5
to wish	祝	9
women's toilets	女厕所	5
wood; a surname	林	2
word	词	3
work, to work	工作	9
work unit	工作单位	8
worker	工人	4
to write	写	3
year	年	4
yellow	黄	7
yesterday	昨(天)	3, (9)
you (singular)	你	6
younger brother	弟弟	5
younger sister	妹妹	5
yuan (unit of Chinese currency)	元, 圆	8
zero	零	4